Georgio Italiano

Georgio Italiano

An American B-25 Pilot's Unlikely Tuscan Adventure.

**Harry D. George and
Harry D. George, Jr.**

©2000 by Harry D. George, Jr.
Book and cover design by Harry D. George, Jr.

No part of this publication may be reproduced, stored in a retrieval system, or transmitted in any form or by any means, electronic, mechanical, recording or otherwise, without the prior written permission of the publisher and author.

Cover design © 2000 by H. D. George, Jr. Cover photos: Behind-the-lines photos courtesy of Renzo Fantoni; H. D. George in B-25 © 1980 by H. D. George, Jr.

Canadian Cataloguing in Publication Data

George, Harry D., 1918-1990.
 Georgio Italiano

ISBN 1-55212-538-6

1. George, Harry D., 1918-1990. 2. World War, 1939-1945--Personal narratives, American. I. George, Harry D., 1949- II. Title.
D811.G464 2001   940.54'8173   C00-911379-7

TRAFFORD

This book was published *on-demand* in cooperation with Trafford Publishing.
On-demand publishing is a unique process and service of making a book available for retail sale to the public taking advantage of on-demand manufacturing and Internet marketing.
On-demand publishing includes promotions, retail sales, manufacturing, order fulfilment, accounting and collecting royalties on behalf of the author.

Suite 6E, 2333 Government St., Victoria, B.C. V8T 4P4, CANADA
 Phone   250-383-6864   Toll-free   1-888-232-4444 (Canada & US)
 Fax   250-383-6803   E-mail   sales@trafford.com
 Web site   www.trafford.com TRAFFORD PUBLISHING IS A DIVISION OF TRAFFORD HOLDINGS LTD.
 Trafford Catalogue #00-0204 www.trafford.com/robots/00-0204.html

10   9   8   7

Dedication

This book is dedicated to the memory of Lt. Rebecca L. George.

It is also dedicated to Col Edward P. Dombrowski, (USAF Ret.) and to the Men of The 487th Bomb Squadron, the 340th Group, and 57th Bomb Wing,

and to my parents, the late Harry D. and Margie E. George.

About the Authors

Harry D. George

Harry D. George (1918-1990) was born and raised in Coatesville, PA. Mr. George worked for Lukens Steel Co. prior to and after WWII, becoming Superintendent of Lukenweld, a subsidiary specializing in fabrication. Thereafter, he joined IMS, International Mill Services, a slag-processing firm with operations in the U.S., Canada, Mexico, Venezuela, and Brazil where he was Vice President Of Operations and subsequently, Vice President of Research. He retired in 1973 at the age of 55. Thereafter, he consulted internationally.

Harry D. George, Jr.

Harry D. George, Jr. (1949-) was raised in Parkesburg, Pa., attended the Peddie School, The University of Pennsylvania, and the Washington College of Law at American University. He practiced corporate law for 23 years and, in 1998, took a mid-life sabbatical to pursue interests in writing and marine photography. He lives in the Chicago area.

Acknowledgments

I wish to thank the following people for their assistance in bringing this project to fruition:

My late parents, Harry D. and Margaret E. George, for their support for my writing and just about everything else I've ever done or tried,

My mother, Margie, especially, for proofing the first drafts and correcting errors in my recollections,

Col. Edward P. Dombrowski (USAF Ret.) for providing background and correcting details in his part of the story,

Renzo Fantoni - for the wartime behind-the-lines photographs, and

Giuseppe and Dina Ferri for hosting our visits, and Beppe for taking me to the story sites and up Georgio's Mountain, and lastly,

The Ferri, Niccoli, and Fantoni families for their efforts in 1944 to assist my father in his survival.

TABLE OF CONTENTS

Chapter 1	At My Father's Knee	1
Chapter 2	The Early Years	11
Chapter 3	Becoming A Pilot	23
Chapter 4	Heading Overseas	47
Chapter 5	Ed and I - Reunion At Alesan	67
Chapter 6	Catch-23	71
Chapter 7	Ed and I - The Jinx	81
Chapter 8	Noble Byars	87
Chapter 9	Mail Call - Letters Home From The Front	91
Chapter 10	Ed and I - The Proof	113
Chapter 11	June 22, 1944	115
Chapter 12	Georgio Italiano	127
Chapter 13	'Sta Sera	141
Chapter 14	Hunted	151
Chapter 15	Garden Gourmet On The Run	165
Chapter 16	Dina!	173
Chapter 17	The Good Life	179
Chapter 18	Ed's Journey South	185
Chapter 19	D-Day in Barberino di Mugello	189
Chapter 20	Anniversary Reunion	197
Chapter 21	Sister Beck and Uncle Harold	207
Chapter 22	Return to Italy	211
Chapter 23	The Measure Of A Woman	217
Chapter 24	Ed and I - One More Time	225
Postscript		229

Photo and Document
Table Of Contents

Plate 1		Map - Story Locations
Plate 2		Map - Bombing Missions
Plate 3	1944	B-25 Schematic Diagram
Plate 4	1944	Mission Photo - Gricigliana Railroad Bridge
Plate 5	1944	7C, The McKinley Jr. High, Going Down
Plate 6	1944	Missing In Action Telegram and Articles
Plate 7	1944	Lt. H. D. George At Caves (June)
Plate 8	1944	*Georgio Itlaliano* At Beppe's
Plate 9	1944	Beppe, Renzo, Georgio, Nello
Plate 10	1944	The Ferri Family
Plate 11	1944	Georgio and The Men and The Women
Plate 12	1944	'Safe' Telegram and Articles
Plate 13	1944	Lt. Rebecca L George: Photo, Articles
Plate 14	1969	Reunion 1969 - The Ferris
Plate 15	1969	Reunion 1969 - The Niccolis
Plate 16	1969	Reunion 1969 - The Fantonis
Plate 17	1944	Reunion 1969 - At The First Cave
Plate 18	1969	Reunion 1969 - At The Padrone's
Plate 19	List	American Military Overseas Cemeteries

Preface

This is one WW II pilot's story - my father's. There are thousands, if not millions, of WWII stories, all worthy of reading. This, however, is a most uncommon one. Many others flew bombing missions and many of those were also shot down. Most who were shot down, however, were either killed or captured. My father was not. He went from cockpit to caveman spending 78 days behind German lines north of Florence, living in mountain caves, foraging for food and water at night, and coming to love, admire and trust three Italian families who made his survival their war effort. During that time, he was 'Georgio,' an Italiano.

But this is not only that story. It is also the story of a young married man obsessed with becoming a pilot, making it through aviation cadet training, then leaving his wife behind to wait for his return while he headed overseas for what was to become the defining adventure of his life...and hers.

This story is as my father told it orally, as he wrote it in letters during the war, and as he wrote it in several short stories afterward. It is his story, in his words. You won't find out what it was like to bomb Tokyo or land on the beaches of Normandy, but you will come away knowing what WWII was like for one man and one woman, from the day he enlisted until the day he was discharged - and then some. It is a story that has never ceased to entertain and amaze both vets and non-vets alike.

INTRODUCTION

I had heard most of my father's war story in bits and pieces over the course of my life - some parts of it numerous times. We talked every day, fished together on weekends, played golf together occasionally, and visited often. I knew his story, or at least most of it, in considerable detail.

During the months of February through June of 1990, when my father was dying of cancer, he told me the complete story from start to finish - the first, last, and only time he ever did so.

He told the complete story then for several reasons. The first reason was to honor *his* heroes one last time – and he had a number of them. That was important to him. He always told his story or any part of it not only to entertain his audience, but to honor his heroes – those who, when their time came, played their parts in the World's greatest and most terrible war to date and did so with courage, heroism, and for some, considerable sacrifice.

The second reason was to make sure that his story was preserved intact with me - with the proper perspectives and the finer nuances. Preserving his story also became important to him in the end.

I am re-telling it here, just as he told it to me in the spring of 1990 - to preserve it, to entertain, and to honor his heroes - just as he did - and to honor him. He was my father, best friend, and hero.

My father's two short stories, *Ed and I* and *The Man Of The Valley* are incorporated as follows*: Ed and I* is set forth in Chapters 5, 7, and 10. *The Man Of The Valley* is incorporated into Chapter 19. My role is to introduce him to you in the first two chapters, to explain a few incidental details along the way (*in italics*), and to wrap things up at the end. The rest is his story - as *he* told it.

Enjoy!

Chapter One
At My Father's Knee

My father, Harry D. George, told his 'good' war stories, the ones about his Italian friends, often. He came from the small town of Coatesville, Pennsylvania, a steel town with a population of about 12,000. His wartime service was widely known and he was asked about it often - even many years after the war. My father was also good storyteller and relished an audience. The stories that he told frequently were the amusing stories and the ones that honored others - never anything about combat or his terror-filled times.

In fact, he didn't begin to talk about the day he was shot down, June 22, 1944, until more than thirty years after the war. Even then, it was only with Ed Dombrowski, the bombardier with whom he was shot down and they didn't discuss it a lot - they had lived it once and that was enough, most of the time.

That didn't mean that the memories of what happened that day were dim – either when my father first began to discuss 'that day' with Ed or when he told his whole story to me in 1990.

For the first ten years after the war, my father relived the events of June 22, 1944 every night in his sleep. Every night, between two and four in the morning, he wrestled that crippled airplane trying to keep it under control, to get it safely out of formation, and to keep it flying level until those who were still alive could get out. He often awoke in the morning exhausted and drenched in sweat.

When I was a young child, the sound of him issuing the order to jump or the sound of him struggling and grunting and straining against the stick and pedals often awakened me. I'd rush into my parents' bedroom to see what was the matter only to find him fast asleep, his arms and legs stiffened like steel, and him twisting and squirming from side to side as he wrestled with that 33,000-pound plane.

There was nothing my mother or I could do. My father could not be awakened and relieved of the ordeal. Neither calling his name nor shaking him worked...and the latter was actually dangerous. My mother and I had both tried shaking him once — and we were both swatted at viciously! He was not about to be distracted or deterred from doing what he had to do - he was still at war. His mind and body were too focused on controlling that plane. He could not be awakened. He would not be awakened. The events of that day simply had to be played out from start to finish – one more time.

My mother cajoled me back to bed. "It'll be over soon," she'd say. "Everything will be all right."

For that night, anyway.

No, the memories of June 22, 1944 weren't dim at all. Every second and every detail of that day were there in his mind, live and in living color and in surround-sound -- forever. It's just that with time, those memories receded to a deeper part of his mind, one that was less insistent on nightly reenactments, and one that, after another twenty or so years, permitted him to talk about it occasionally.

In late January of 1990, just two months after his last clear X-ray, my father was diagnosed with lung cancer. The prognosis was not good. In those two months, it had already advanced too far – too far to be operable and too far to be curable – just like it had with his mother, Elsie, in 1941 at precisely the same age.

I received a phone call from my mother immediately after they had met with the doctor and heard the diagnosis and prognosis. She didn't want to talk, but wanted me to call the doctor. She wanted to be sure that they had heard everything correctly – that *she,* the nurse, had heard everything correctly.

My father heard what he needed to hear - two to six months. With chemotherapy. That's all he needed to know and he tuned the rest out. The other details were unimportant.

My mother wanted to remember everything and couldn't. She was reeling from the shock. She knew the prognosis, but the rest was a blur. It was the only time I ever knew her to miss a medical detail. But she did. And she wanted me to call the doctor.

I called the doctor immediately and heard the same thing: my father had cancer – small cell lung cancer which had spread to his liver or kidneys, I no longer remember which. I just remember that chemotherapy could buy him time, some precious time, but it could not change the final outcome. There was a chance that the cancer could be stopped or cured, but that chance was remote at best. In something between two and six months, he would be dead. That was it. The future was known. There was no sugar coating, at least none that I could find. Two to six months. Period.

I lived in Chicago, some 750 miles away from my parents' home in Exton, Pa. I was an only child. My parents would need support during this. I was the only one who could provide it. I adjusted my work schedule. I worked from Monday through Wednesday of the following week - ten straight work days and then I took four days off and drove home. Flying would have been easier, but with a wife and two kids, the expense of that every two weeks was just too much. We drove home every other weekend.

I made the twelve-hour drives home to Pennsylvania beginning at midnight, Wednesday nights, and arriving at home at noon on Thursdays. Then on Sunday, I left Pennsylvania at six p.m. and arrived at home in Chicago Monday morning at six a.m. – then caught the 6:50 train to work – beginning the process all over again. I spent three and a half days at home every two weeks over the next four and a half months. It was the least I could do. In fact, it was all I could do.

On my visits home, I helped my mother with details - largely handling insurance bills and running errands – and spelling her on caring for my father. My wife and kids accompanied me on those trips.

It might sound depressing tending to one's dying father, but it was not. My father was still my father - he was a good guy to spend time with. He did not like to make people uneasy and didn't. Quite the opposite. He made spending time with him enjoyable. He made a point to put people at their ease. Always. Even in this distressing circumstance.

In 1968, my mother had suffered a near-fatal heart attack. She was pronounced dead on three separate occasions – at home by the attending physician (one of our neighbors), by the paramedics in the ambulance, and at the hospital where she was Dead-On-Arrival. But they zapped her one last time with the defibrillator and she came back. Clearly, her time had not yet come.

She was hospitalized for six weeks – the standard treatment in the late 60's. I was, at nineteen, too young to fully comprehend the magnitude of those events as they unfolded.

I learned that she had a heart attack when I returned home from work from my summer job. I rushed to the Bryn Mawr Hospital from our home in Valley Forge. The drive took me 25 minutes – double the ambulance's time. And I sped! My father was already there. Her heart was beating again, but that was about it. There were twelve hellish hours until she came out of the coma, but once she started talking, I believed that the episode was over. I firmly believed that she would live.

My father, on the other hand, understood the continued precariousness of the situation only too well. There were some things he wanted to say to her, needed to say to her, but couldn't. They were just too intense, too emotional and the timing as not right - her health was too fragile and would remain so for some time. So, in the dead of the night one night when she was still in the hospital, he gathered his wits and his strength and made an audio tape for her to hear upon her arrival home. He was talking to a machine, not her. That was easier for him somehow.

He asked me to listen to the tape in advance. He wanted to be sure that it hit its mark. It did. I think he also wanted me to hear exactly how he felt about her. I did.

After she was home and settled, he played the tape for her – while sitting there holding her hand. What needed to be said was said. And appreciated.

I had the same problem in 1990, but with him. Some things had to be said. It hits you like a brick when you hear a doctor pronounce a death sentence on your father. Especially so when your father is also your best friend. I had a lot of intense emotions to deal with and it was my time to be a rock for him just as he had always been that for everyone else.

When I got home from work that day, I went to my study on the second floor and paced. I paced all over the whole upstairs of the house. For hours. I could not sit still. I cried a fair amount during that time as well. I hadn't done that since I had broken my collar bone falling off a swing at age five, but I did it then. I felt a profound sense of loss immediately.

My emotions were getting in the way – in the way of my functioning. They had to be dealt with right then and there and then put aside. I had to be able to function during this – for myself and for my father and mother.

I sat down and wrote my father a letter – to be read upon his arrival home from the hospital just as his tape had been for my mother. I told him what I wanted him to hear and what I thought he needed to hear.

To paraphrase, it said this:

There's really nothing that needs to be said or done between us that hasn't already been said or done, but sometimes it is 'fitting and proper' (a phrase from Lincoln's Gettysburg Address - and he was a major fan of Lincoln) to reiterate. This is one of those times.

One doesn't get to choose one's father; biology takes care of that, but if I had the opportunity to choose my father, I would have chosen you. What one can choose in this life are your friends and I have always been heartened that as adults, we had become friends, best friends. I never really knew where the father-son relationship ended and the friendship began, but that was one of the better things about it.

I reiterated many of the things and experiences he had given me - and it was a long list – and noted that in doing so, he had given me more happiness than he could ever imagine. I noted that my children, his grandchildren, had been very lucky - there never was a more doting and involved grandfather. I closed, of course, by telling him that I loved him immensely.

I mailed him the letter so that he would have it when he arrived home from the hospital in two days - after the first chemo treatment.

We never discussed that letter. Just as he and my mother had never discussed his tape. It just wasn't done -- especially not by a man of his generation. But he kept that letter within his reach from the time he received it until he died five months later. If he changed rooms, the letter changed rooms. Often it just sat, on the end table or on the night stand or bureau. Often he re-read it -- when he was alone or thought he was. He understood. I understood. There was no need to discuss it. And I had understood what to do and how to do it – from him. He hit his mark. I had hit mine.

Despite all of the education I had, and I had a pretty top-drawer one, it seems that everything I really needed to know, I learned from my father – at his knee.

But, as I said earlier, he made things easy on others. His last months were no different. What was, just was. He believed that every day he was alive after June 22, 1944 was a bonus. That didn't change during the Spring of 1990.

During that time, he talked to and played with his grandchildren. He still went to The Diner for his morning B. S. session with the guys, the old guys, the good guys. (It was a coffee klatch and gossip session, but one didn't dare call it that. Women gossiped. Men B.S.'d.) He still played 'Quarters' and Yahtzee with my mother. And he still told jokes and stories. He even went to his 55th high school reunion in a wheelchair two weeks before he died. He was weak, gaunt, and almost hairless from the chemo, but he went and had a high old time.

He went in a wheelchair to make things easier for himself and for others. It was the first time he had ever used a wheelchair. As weak as he was getting, he still did everything under his own power - a point of honor with him. He just did less and slower. Until that night – that night he used a wheelchair.

He knew many would stay away from someone in his condition. Cancer had that effect on people. Without a wheelchair, he would have been tied to one table and would have had few visitors. But with a wheelchair, he could circulate -- circulate to see all of his old friends, to make his familiar smart remarks, to tell jokes, and to entertain and amuse...and to put people at their ease. And he did. He was his old self that evening -- his last good time 'out'. He was just sitting down instead of standing. No one minded. Really. They enjoyed! He enjoyed!

On my first visit home after the diagnosis, my father hinted that he wanted to tell some of his stories, his war stories, one more time. I didn't need more than a hint. I liked listening to him tell stories, any stories, but especially his war stories. I asked him to tell them to me again. Eventually, his purposes became clear.

He always started the story with the same opening line, "There I was at 10,000 feet over Italy..." He would then mention being shot down as if it were an inconsequential detail, and proceed to recount some of aspect of his three months on the ground behind German lines in Italy in the summer of 1944. His last telling began exactly the same way. After the first line, however, this telling, was different. It included June 22, 1944 and a whole lot more.

His last telling took a long time. It occupied much of the time we spent together over the succeeding months. It was time well spent for both of us. He had a story to tell and his heroes to honor -- and he didn't want them or anything they had done forgotten. That was fair enough. For me, it was some more time at my father's knee listening to him tell stories and I enjoyed that. It was easy.

When I was a small child, he was not an active father. He was not at all comfortable with very small children (until he had grandchildren). Little people were an enigma to him. I think that he grew up when he was four years old when his father died. With that, he seemed to have forgotten what the carefree part of a child's life was like.

What he did do with me when I was very young was to read poetry. He read from a huge anthology which was covered with a maroon, marbleized paper jacket. My favorite was *The Cataract Song,* a lyrical and rhythmical poem about a brook. I had no idea what a cataract was and, although I'm sure he explained it to me way back then, I mentally heard it as *The Cadillac Song*. It was just fine that way too. Nice cars, Cadillacs.

And he told me stories - stories about his days as a child in Coatesville, Pa. He and his friends named themselves the 'Olive Street Wildcats.' They were Coatesville's answer to the "Our Gang' of movie fame. My father was most definitely Spanky - the instigator, but in Alfalfa's body.

I was a willing listener to both the poetry and the stories. I sat either on his knee or on the floor next to it.

This final story time would be different. I was bigger - a lot bigger - and he was smaller and weaker. Sitting on his knee was out. Sitting on the floor by his knee would have worked, but I felt too grown-up for that. So I sat on the couch opposite his favorite chair.

By the end of the story in May, he was wheelchair-bound. We often sat knee-to-knee so that talking wouldn't be as difficult for him or hearing him as difficult for me. Oddly, being knee-to-knee felt quite the same as being at his knee as a child -- regardless of how thin, weak, and bony that knee had become. He was still my father and still telling me stories.

I was not alone in getting some knee time during those last months. My daughter, Jennifer, who was fourteen at the time, wanted to go in to spend time with him as well – extra time, not just what time she got to spend with him on one of our visits home.

My kids, Jen and Harry, III, were fourteen and twelve. I saw no reason not to tell them what was going on. There really wasn't any way to hide it from them anyway. I'd taken them to funerals since they were old enough to walk. Death is part of life and there is no reason to delay learning about it, learning the rituals. Better to learn how to deal with it when it involves remote relatives than all at once with close ones. My kids learned the process at an early age. They knew the drill.

Jen wanted to spend two weeks with my parents helping out. That was her way of saying good-bye. It was one I knew he would understand and appreciate. Her mother objected, but her objections fell on deaf ears - two sets of them, Jen's and mine. Jen went. For two weeks. In May. Near the end.

That kid can do anything between now and her dying day and she will never do anything that is either better, more caring, or more noble. Or that could shake my loyalty to her one bit. Spending two weeks with her dying grandfather was courageous! And it was loyal.

My father measured people by how they handled things when the chips were down – a perspective he brought home from the war – and one that he lived thereafter. His chips were down and Jen was right there beside him – literally. She was very much like him.

Jen stayed there for the two weeks and pitched in. She did chores; she listened to stories; and sometimes she just sat there and held his hand.

And sometimes, she straightened his ass out. Yeah, this 'kid' of fourteen straightened the old war horse himself out! Things were tough on both of my parents. My mother, the nurse and organizer of everything, was organizing him and his death, perhaps a bit too much, perhaps not. He never did take too well to being ordered around by anyone. Some major friction was developing.

When my father was out of line in remarks he made to my mother, Jen told him so in no uncertain terms. And he listened, apologized, and changed. When Mom was out of line in her handling of him, Jen told her too. And she listened, apologized, and changed. Jen wasn't just there supporting him, she made those two weeks a whole lot better for everyone. She made it easier for them to be themselves with each other at a time when they needed that. That was truly a fine gift. The finest.

And my father told stories to Jen too. Stories about when she was little - when they used to take long walks together and he would let her pull leaves out of rain gutters – something no parent would ever allow, but something in which grandparent and grandchild took particular delight. You never knew what you might find! He told her stories of their New Year's Eve bashes – grand parties all of them! (Even if they were only attended by my parents and my kids.) He knew what stories to tell and how to tell them.

My father always made being with him easy. And he liked to tell stories. We all had some time at my father's knee – even in those last days.

Chapter Two
The Early Years

I knew my parents as they were after the war. My father was ambitious, studious, disciplined, controlled, and steely. He was determined to make something of himself, to get ahead. He took correspondence courses regularly. He read voraciously – Book-Of-The Month Club and other novels - but also such heavier fare as Churchill's *Valiant Years*, *Battles and Leaders* (of the Civil War), and Sandburg's *Lincoln*, with a little of Robert Frost's poetry thrown in for good measure. He worked long hours and he gave time to the community – serving on the school board and heading the local sewer authority. He also fished regularly – sometimes locally, but starting in 1948 and continuing until 1989, he took an annual week-long fishing trip to Canada. From the time I was fourteen, I joined him on those adventures.

My mother was the typical wife – at home raising me, but also becoming a Cub Scout Den Mother, and doing the neighborhood nursing.

As my father recounted his war story for the last time, I tried to put it more in context than I ever had before. I silently reviewed what I knew about both of my parents' lives up to that point so that I could see their story more as it happened to them and less as it was told to me long after the fact.

I knew a fair amount about my parents' lives through high school.

My father's family had been poor, but as he often said, they didn't know it or feel it. Many other people were also poor. Their poverty started in 1923 with the death of his father in March. My father was four years old.

My father had very few memories of his father - two to be exact. He remembered his father leading parades of his four kids around the house on the Fourth of July, while playing *The Stars and Stripes Forever* on the trombone. His father was a Superintendent in the steel mill, but his passion was music. He was a virtuoso trombone player who, according to family legend, auditioned for the Maestro himself, John Philip Sousa, in early 1923, was accepted into Sousa's post-Marine Corps Band, but before he could join them, took sick and died.

My father's only other memory of his father was of the viewing and funeral. The viewing was held at their home in late March of 1923. The line of people who had come to pay their respects was very long and the front door left open. It was cold in the house and my father complained to his mother about the open door – it was making his Daddy too cold! Not a lot of memories.

My father went to work shortly thereafter – as soon as he turned five in May of 1923, the minimum age for newspaper delivery boys. He took over his older brother's paper route when Fred, then seven, moved up to a more substantial one. The Depression had little or no effect on my father's family. Their Depression started in 1923 when his father died, not in 1929 when it began for the rest of the country. Everyone in the family pitched in. Everyone had to. Even my father at five. His earnings were turned over to his mother in their entirety. It just had to be.

My father's oldest brother was his half-brother, Walt Carlin. He and my father had the same mother, Elsie. Elsie's first husband deserted her and Walt when he was a newborn. They had been married no more than two years. She moved back in with her widowed mother and raised her son. After seven years, Elsie filed for divorce. It was granted a year later – a real stigma for a woman at the turn of the 20th Century.

Walt was a grown man of twenty when my father was born. He served in World War I, in the ambulance corps, I believe – quite Hemingway-esque - only Walt served in France, not Italy. Walt became my father's role model.

Walt sold insurance and had his own agency. He was tall, outgoing, and personable. He did quite well at the insurance business and, in the mid-1930's bought a 120-acre farm which he and his wife, Mary, and their boys, Walt, Bill, and Richard, started to restore. He became County Treasurer and later, Clerk of Orphan's Court. As a substitute father figure, my father couldn't have asked for a better one. And my father clearly emulated him. Not only were they the same height, they had much the same manner about them.

With the death of her second husband, my father's father, Elsie took a hard look at her young children. She had to be realistic in how she raised them. She took a unique tack with raising my father. She wanted to be sure that he would become self-reliant, so, from the time he started working, he had few rules and no curfew. He had to behave properly in the house, but he came and went on his schedule. The only requirement – he had to stop and tell her that he was home whenever he came in – regardless of the hour. He became street-smart long before that description was conceived or the phrase coined. Elsie mothered his brother, Fred, more closely. My father, she turned loose. They were different. They got different treatment.

My father did not take school all that seriously. He was exceptionally bright, but just did what was necessary to get by and only studied what intrigued him. Not a whole lot did. The capsule description in his high school year book was this: "He knows so little, but knows it so fluently!" He was fluent. He always had a superb vocabulary and always told a good story, but school was not his *forte*.

His mother supported the family by becoming a seamstress. She worked hard and with help from Walt, from my grandfather's two children from his first marriage, French and Beck, and with help from her two youngest children, Fred and my father, she was able to keep the household together – even through the Depression.

One brief aside – my grandfather George, my father's father, was a widower. His first wife, Ada, died in 1911 shortly after the birth of their last child, Rebecca. Rebecca was always known as 'Beck.' With two young children to raise, my grandfather needed help - daycare we call it today. He moved in with Ada's mother and her sister, Elsie. At that point in time, Elsie had been divorced for seven years. Her son, Walt, was nearly grown. It was quite natural that she became a surrogate mother to French and Beck, her niece and nephew, and that she and my father's father would eventually fall in love and marry.

My father didn't talk much about his youth except for his friends ('The Olive Street Wildcats'), the kind man who paid for his membership to the local YMCA for ten years, his sister, Beck, and his mother. Despite the fact that Elsie gave him a very long leash, she was strict when it came to proper behavior at home. He viewed her as a Saint. He revered her. She was his rock.

In his teens, my father followed in his father's footsteps with the trombone – or tried to. There was only one problem, he didn't get the trombone gene. He was a fine technician, but no more. He was not tone deaf, but not far from it either – and the trombone requires an ear in addition to technique. He played in several bands – dance bands put together by friends.

My father spent much of his young life bedeviling his sister, Beck. She was eight years older than my father and a very serious young woman. When they walked home from church together on Sundays, he was the clown. And in his Sunday finery no less! That drove Beck wild – which only made him exaggerate his antics even more.

One rainy day when he was about ten years old and killing time on the front porch, he noticed Beck in the living room reading.

"Hey, Beck!" he called, "Did you ever see it rain sideways?"

She got up from her chair and went to the side window whereupon she noticed that something was, indeed, making it rain, or rather 'stream,' sideways. It was my father – taking a leak off the side of the front porch. She was furious! With that, he was pleased!

Such was their relationship - typical big-sister-and-impish-baby-brother stuff. His bedeviling of her, as annoying as it certainly was for her, was really a sign of his great affection – and there was a very great affection between them. When she became a nurse, the first money she earned went to buy my father his own trombone. That's how the family was – a set of rather different characters, but ones who counted on each other and who did for each other when the chips were down.

French was my father's second eldest brother – also a half brother, but with the same father. French was ten years older and was my grandfather's first son. He too worked to help support the family. He worked as a cook, bricklayer, butcher, carpenter, and seemingly just about anything else that paid reasonably well. He and my father weren't especially close, but they were still brothers. French was quiet and unassuming, but with a very wry, under-his-breath sense of humor. Later in life, he told how, when my father was born, he had to help change my father's diapers.

"I resented having to help change Harry's diapers. He was 'the baby' and the world seemed to revolve around him. Changing his diapers was not a pleasant task. He produced a lot of shit.....still does."

That was French – you always had to wait for the whispered zinger at the end.

French became a welder at the steel mill. He remained there for forty years – until his retirement at age sixty-five. His passion in life was sailing. First he had a twenty-one foot sailboat. In the 1950's, as a welder with considerable seniority, he received 13 weeks' annual paid vacation. He took the bulk of that vacation in the summer and worked at the local YMCA's summer camp on the upper end of the Chesapeake Bay. He kept his sailboat there. He spent every afternoon sailing, often with his wife, Laura. The rest of the time they both worked at the camp – she as a cook and he as an 'everything' man.

As French was approaching retirement, he and a friend designed and built a steel-hulled 43-foot ketch which they then sailed on the Chesapeake during the summers and took to Florida for the winters. "The Ark,' as I referred to it, took them a dozen years to build -- during which I referred to him as 'Uncle Noah' and asked him repeatedly when the flood was coming. He got a kick out of that. "Not until we're finished! Read your Bible!" was his reply. They got a dozen years out of that boat before old age caught up with them and the boat had to be sold.

The last of my father's siblings was his full brother, Fred. Fred was two years older than my father. He was serious and straight-forward. And good-hearted in the extreme. Still is. Physically, they were quite similar – similar voices and one could always look at the one's face and see the other's in it. There were, however, two major differences. The first was about four inches in height. Fred is five-foot-nine and my father was six-one. The second difference was that Fred was a superb athlete – a star soccer player in high school. My father was not exceptional.

In high school, my father wanted to play football. At six-one and one hundred and thirty pounds, he was not the ideal football candidate –

especially not for a very serious high school program. Mill towns take their football very seriously! Very!

When the first round of cuts was made, my father's name was on the list. That was fine. He just kept going to practices anyway. When the second round of cuts was made, his name was on it again. That was fine too. He continued to go to practices. When the third round of cuts were made, his name was on the list again – this time at the top of the list in bold letters. After practice that day, the coach called him in and told him that he had been cut...and cut not once, but three times!

"I know," was my father's reply, "and if you cut me one more time, I'm going to quit your damn team!" He was not easily deterred when he had his heart set on something. But he was cut from the football team and that was that.

In his post-high-school days, my father was known to drink a bit and occasionally got locked up for it. They did things like that back then, but generally one was only kept in jail until one sobered up. Then you were released. There were no charges filed or records made. But my father didn't like it.

His jail-breaking technique was to become so incessantly and obnoxiously conversant that his jailers would just drive him home rather than endure his ramblings for an entire night. As he put it, "I've been thrown out of more jails than most people ever get thrown into."

That was as far as he would ever go in doing anything wrong or illegal. He had his own compass and standards. Doing a bit of drinking and having a good time were within his limits. Anything else was not.

I guess the best way to put it is that my father was incorrigible – bright and charming, but most definitely incorrigible.

After high school, he dated a fair amount – mostly nurses. I think that was in part a desire to find someone similar to Beck and because I think that he figured that they weren't prudes. I think he also admired their strength. He could not handle hospitals at all. Hospitals made him faint. In fact, that's how he met my mother. He fainted.

He was in the hospital to visit his mother who had some minor surgery. Elsie was about the only person he would set foot inside a hospital to see. But before he got to her room, he fainted.

My mother was on duty on that floor and rushed to see what had happened. He was 'out' and sprawled across the floor. She knelt over him. He didn't respond. She got some smelling salts and waved them under his nose. He came around.

"Hi, gorgeous! You, I've got to meet!" were his words of introduction – from a prone position on the hospital floor. Before getting up, he asked her out for coffee and she agreed.

He visited his mother that day and when my mother came off duty, they went downtown for coffee. There was only one thing wrong – he didn't have the money to pay for it. My mother did. She paid.

My father was not the least bit embarrassed. "I just had to get to know you. I wasn't thinking about money. Just you. You're so pretty, you overwhelmed me!"

It was The Depression and not having money was common. And he had made a very charming recovery. He was quite proud of it, actually. And it was true. He thought she was just about the prettiest girl he had ever seen. My mother was both charmed and intrigued. But that was the first and last time that she paid.

My father didn't go to college. When one doesn't have the money for coffee, college is more than a little beyond one's means.

My father had been offered a full scholarship to college, but turned it down. There was a string attached to it and he didn't know if he could handle that string. The scholarship was offered by the same man who had paid for his YMCA membership from the time his father died until his teens. There was a string attached to that as well - the same string. He could have an annual YMCA membership on the condition that if he were ever able to do the same thing for someone else, he was obligated to do so. At five, that sounded like a good deal to him and he took it (and he kept his part of the deal many times over later in his life). At eighteen, a college scholarship on the same terms was, perhaps, too big an obligation to carry around for the rest of his life. He took his obligations seriously. He said no.

Finally, he got a job in the local steel mill, Lukens Steel. He had gone to the President's Office and applied for a job. It was the singular time in his life that he traded on his father's name. The President of the steel company had been one of his father's best friends when they were young boys in the 1880's. The President saw him, but had to tell him that there were no jobs to be had at that time. He was sorry. But he remembered my father's father very fondly.

About two weeks later, a car and driver appeared in front of the family home on Olive Street. The driver came to the door and asked for "Albert George." Elsie told the driver that there was no Albert George at that address. There wasn't. In fact, there wasn't even an Albert George in the whole town. Albert, my father's grandfather, was long since dead.

My father overheard the conversation and interjected that there certainly was an Albert George and he was him. The President of the mill had confused my father's name with his grandfather's name. He thought that my father had been named for his grandfather.

"Yes, I'm Albert. What can I do for you." he asked the driver.

"The President found a job for you," the driver replied. "Report to the Strode Avenue Office on Monday. The President really admired your father. He said to tell you that it was the least he could do."

"Tell him Albert says 'thank you very much.' I'll be there first thing Monday morning," my father replied.

So he was 'Albert' George for his first year at the mill. But he had a job. He had money. Those were very important then. He could continue dating my mother.

Just before the war, he applied for an opening in the Time-Study Department. The 'in' thing in management at that time was time study – watching what people did and how they did it, then devising ways to simplify and improve it – to make people more efficient, more like machines. Units of action were called 'Therbligs,' named for their inventors, a husband and wife team by the name of Gilbreth. Therblig is Gilbreth spelled backwards (or thereabouts). The only requirement for the job was typing.

My father couldn't type, but said that he could. He got the job.

His desk abutted his boss's desk. Hiding his lack of typing skill was a challenge. He typed a lot of gibberish when his boss was seated across from him. When his boss was away from his desk, my father did his serious typing. It was hunt-and-peck at first, but eventually, he became proficient. He wrote good reports and made good suggestions. His work was noticed. He was 'promotable.'

He and my mother dated for about a year before they decided to get married. My father made only one promise to my mother.

"I can't promise you much in the way of material things, but I can promise you one thing – being married to me will never be dull."

That must have been sufficient for my mother because she accepted his proposal. And he kept his promise – being married to him never was dull – often much to my mother's chagrin, but she had no room to complain – he had been forthright about it with her.

They announced their engagement at Walt and Mary's farm at the family Christmas Eve in 1938. There was no timetable set. They were just engaged. When they had the funds to setup housekeeping on their own, they would get married. In October of 1939, they were satisfied that the time had come.

They agreed on a small wedding – just a few people and a minister. Actually, the wedding was to consist solely of my father and mother, his brother, Fred, as Best Man, and my mother's sister, Audrey, as Maid of Honor. That was it – four people. Afterward, my mother's grandmother would host a small reception at her home.

Then my father started telling people that they were getting married. His friends all wanted to come, so he invited them. When my parents arrived at the church at the appointed hour, it was half full – on one side, the groom's side. There were several hundred 'invitees.' My mother's side was empty – as it was supposed to be.

Why she didn't blow a cork on that day, I'll never know. But she didn't. Their marriage never was dull and that started on their wedding day. As he said, it didn't cost anything to have them sit in the church. And it didn't cost (him) anything to have them back to the reception.

As I said – he was incorrigible.

They took a short honeymoon to Washington, D.C. and began married life in an apartment in West Chester, Pa. where my mother worked briefly as a nurse at the hospital there.

As far as I can tell, their early married life was extremely happy. My mother changed jobs – returning to Coatesville Hospital where she had trained. She occasionally took some private-duty assignments. Several were for the Copeland family who had a large farm west of Coatesville. She nursed several of the older Copelands through their last days – her first experience with hospice-type nursing – experience that served her well in 1990. They eventually rented a house from the Copeland family. It was in Westwood, Pa. and close to the Copeland farm. They were set.

Then in 1941, Elsie developed cancer and died. That devastated my father. She had been the anchor of his life. And she was gone – forever. As my mother said, it was the one and only time in her life that she saw my father cry. And he cried like a baby – privately, in his bedroom, but also uncontrollably for quite some time.

But life goes on. And it did.

My mother's youth was radically different from my father's. She was the eldest of four children. She was the big sister that the others bedeviled – which is probably where she developed the skills necessary to cope with my father. She was also the big sister to whom her siblings all turned in times of crisis. And she never let them down -- the 'Big Sister Complex.'

She missed one year of elementary school when she was quarantined with pleurisy. She lived in one room of their house and no one was allowed to visit. She could not leave the room and no one could come in. She was seven or eight. Her meals were delivered to her through a slit that was cut in the wall and opened only for that purpose. I've often tried to imagine what it would be like to be seven years old and to go for that amount of time with no human contact - no touching, no playing, no fun whatsoever. It was not a pleasant experience, but it apparently steeled my mother. She could endure anything after that.

Her family moved frequently. Her father managed grocery stores and was constantly trying to improve himself by changing jobs. They did well enough financially, but there was little stability. There was no one place that was home.

She was born in Coatesville, moved to Christiana when she was five, to Williamsport when she was six, and to Lancaster, Pa. when she was ten or eleven. They stayed there until she was graduated from high school. It was as close as she would come to 'home,' but she hadn't grown up with all of her classmates, so there was always some distance between them.

Her grandfather had opened a drug store in Lancaster. Her father joined him in managing it. They lost it in the Depression – something my mother always blamed on Franklin Roosevelt. He was no friend of the small businessman, at least according to her.

Their family life was not easy either. Her parents were both hotheads. They fought often and separated frequently. The children took sides. My mother and the next oldest, her brother, Ray, sided with their father and usually left with him. The two youngest, Audrey and Donald, sided with their mother and stayed with her. My mother became the peace-maker.

All sides of my mother's family were German. Her father's family had been Mennonite (a Pennsylvania Dutch sect) until her grandparents' generation. While they had come to the U.S. in the mid-1600's, their German roots were still evident almost three hundred years later. They were stern people and everyone always claimed to have a monopoly on the correct answer or analysis to any problem or situation. Put any two of them in a room for more than five minutes and you had a fight. That's just how they were - opinionated, loud, and obnoxious...and one always trying to be cuter and smarter than the next. My mother's reaction to that environment was to become quiet and compassionate. She was the peacemaker and care giver. She became so at a young age and remained that way throughout her life.

My mother's family's connection to their heritage was in stark contrast to my father's. The Georges came from Wurtemburg, Germany in 1742. By the 1850's, they were fully Americanized and had completely forgotten their country of origin. It wasn't until another sixty or seventy years later that my father's Aunt Mary did some genealogical research and re-discovered the German connection – and even then, no one believed her. David Lloyd George was Prime Minister of Great Britain. The Georges had to be British! German? It just couldn't be. And if it were true, who would want to admit to it? They were the villains in World War I – not an ethnic origin that one could proudly claim. And they didn't. Still don't. The Georges are American. Period.

In high school, my mother was an average student. What she enjoyed was participating in the musical theater productions. She sang in the chorus. She was counting the days until graduation – when she could strike out on her own and escape the constant bickering and tension at home.

When she was graduated from high school, she left home to go to nursing school at Coatesville Hospital. She lived with her grandparents who had re-located there. There was considerably more peace in their house. She did well at nursing school and was hired by the hospital upon her graduation.

On December 7, 1941, my parents, then married just over two years, were to go to Walt and Mary's for supper. For no reason in particular, they decided to walk the six miles to the farm instead of driving. It had snowed overnight and it was a gorgeous day – bright and sunny with new snow covering the hills and trees. They had a lovely, romantic walk together through the snow.

When they arrived at the farm just after noon, they heard the news that Pearl Harbor had been attacked. The country was at war.

And it is now time to adjourn - to my father's knee.

Chapter Three
Becoming A Pilot

There I was...at 10,000 feet over Italy...

No. Let's start at the beginning - in October of 1942.

I always wanted to be a pilot. Don't know why. Just did.

In October of 1942, the Air Corps announced that they would start taking married men as Aviation Cadets. I worked for Lukens Steel Company in Coatesville, Pa. and had a draft-exempt job. The day after they made the announcement, my childhood friend, Rich Orth, who was also married and had a deferment, and I signed up. Neither one of us discussed it with our wives. We just did it. We both just wanted to be pilots and that was that.

Initially, your mother was quite aggravated with me. I had just turned our lives upside-down without any consultation with her. But it didn't take long for her to switch into a supportive role. The whole country was immersed in the war effort and one couldn't take a position against it in any context. She ended up being tremendously supportive of my obsession to become a pilot.

I was called up on January 28th of 1943.

Ha! When I was young, I loved my sack time. Sleep and I, it seemed, were made for each other. The day I was to catch the train and report for duty, I overslept – by two hours - well past the time for the train! I got up, got dressed, and rushed to the station all in about twenty minutes. I didn't know what I was going to do, but as fate would have it, the train was running about two and a half hours late. I made it and the Army never knew the difference!

I went through Basic Training in Florida and then was sent to Concord State Teachers College in Athens, West Virginia for 6 weeks of academic training.

When I discovered my father's letters home from the service, I also discovered a different person - someone far younger, far less sophisticated, and far less disciplined and controlled than the father who had raised me. When I was born, he was thirty-one and a combat veteran. He often seemed more like fifty. He was thoughtful, deliberative, and fair – good qualities all. But he was also distant - never overtly emotional - and that made being his son a bit of a challenge, especially in my younger years.

But here, in his letters, he was very young - even at twenty-five and married. He was enthusiastic. He was even downright effusive at times! I'd always figured that someone very similar to this 'new' person had been in there somewhere. Now I knew! There had been. He had been to war in the interim and had done a lot of learning and growing up, but he had been young once...and had been far more open and effusive – and far more emotional.

He wrote to his older brother, Walt, and Walt's wife, Mary, during training. While Walt was a father figure and role model, he was also a brother and a World War I vet - someone he could talk to openly.

From Basic Training:

>Sunday, Feb 14, 1943

>Dear Walt and Mary,

>I sure like Army life and its doing me a world of good. This is sure some country down here. I can look out of my hotel window and see all the coconut trees I want. I've been in swimming a couple of times and both the beach and the water are fine. I don't know how the food was in your war, but in mine it is swell. We get a good variety and all we want to eat, the only thing in the eating line that we don't have is butter. I have not tasted any since we got down here. We use apple butter

and jam instead, but I can honestly say I don't miss it at all. We have gotten three needles so far and get another one tomorrow, but as yet I have had no reaction. All our meals are served cafeteria style and all we do is get an aluminum tray and let them fill it up.

How is Walter making out with the draft? I told Margie if she ever wanted to know anything about the house, etc. that she had better talk to you because I don't think she's ever had much experience along those lines before. You can tell Richard that I sure would like a letter from him as he supposed to be quite good at that sort of stuff. If you ever have to get in touch with me by phone, I think that by just giving the operator my address and telling her I am staying at the Shoreham Hotel, I can be reached with very little trouble. Well, I am going to close now folks. Write when you can as I would sure like to hear from you.

So Long,

Harry

Walter and Richard are Walt's sons. The Shoreham Hotel in Miami? Now that's Basic Training you could sell!

From Concord State Teachers College, Athens, West Virginia: Pre-Cadet Training:

Sunday, March 28, 1943

Dear Walt, Mary, Walter, Bill, and Richard,

It has been quite a while since I received your letter but this is really the first chance I have had to answer it as we are kept going just about all the time. The studies here are pretty tough and we have to keep studying just about all the time we have to spare. The course in Physics is about the toughest of all them and I spend a good deal of time studying this. I doubt very much if I will be able to get home for quite a while because our schedule is based on so many days to cover the work and they just won't let us figure on missing any studies for any reason.

Was glad to hear Richard got himself a pair of Grade A riding britches and you can tell him when I get home I'll teach him how to ride. We have started cross country runs now and if you have never seen the hills they have down here, I doubt if could appreciate our efforts. It seems that they go straight up and then straight down on the other side and when you run four or five miles over them you really feel a little tired and I'm not kidding the least bit. At first, I thought it was going to kill me, but I'm getting pretty used to it now and about ten minutes after we are through, I feel back on the beam again.

Was sure glad to hear that boys are making out so well and especially with the chickens because that's one thing I really go for. The food here is very good and there seems to be plenty of it. I have become quite a coffee drinker since I arrived here. We have it with every meal and I drink two cups for breakfast, dinner, and supper.

Well, folks, I am just about out of news so I['m] going to close and write a couple more letters as I'm really behind in my correspondence.

Love,

Harry

P.S. I start to fly this week.

Post Card from Nashville, TN on the way to Pre-Flight Training:

Dear Walt and Mary et al,

Just a note to let you know I have moved. Will be here about a month. This is a real army camp with no luxuries at all. Will let you know as soon as I'm classified.

Harry

Then came Pre-Flight training at Maxwell Field in Montgomery, Alabama and Primary Flight Training in Jackson, Tennessee. I was great at the academic side of flying -- actually I was at the top of my class -- but I had great trouble getting any sort of feel for actually flying airplanes. I was beginning to think that I was just too methodical, but I could not and would not accept failure.

My epiphany occurred one morning when my Primary flight instructor, Bill Clark, roused me at 5 am. He told me to get dressed and to meet him at the field. I did in a flash although this procedure seemed rather odd. We climbed into the Stearman ST-17, a bi-plane trainer. He took the command position. I climbed into the student position. We took off. He was silent. There was no instruction.

About 20 minutes later, we landed at a remote field. He got out. I got out. He said, "OK, George, today you're either going to become a pilot....or die trying. Get back in the plane and start practicing take-offs and landings."

"If I die, tell them I died a hero's death," I replied and headed for the plane.

The only real tough parts of flying are take-offs and landings, called 'transition'. Once you're in the air, it's very similar to driving a car -- except that planes have a few more controls and you can roll a plane over and keep going, but you can't with a car. I had no trouble with take-offs. To take-off, one simply has to go through the checklist thoroughly, put the power to the engine, reach air speed, and gently lift up on the wheel or stick.

Landing is a different matter. You have to get on a straight line with runway and get down on it soon enough to stop the plane before the runway ends. You are also cutting power not applying it – you have less control. And there are also cross winds to deal with and the attitude of the plane -- and judging the distance to the ground.

I climbed into the front seat of the ST-17. I was both petrified and relieved. I was petrified of dying and relieved that there was a deadline and today was it.

I went through the checklist. I liked the ST-17's. They were rugged planes and were quite stable in the air. I had about 20 hours in them, but none soloing. My take-offs had all been fine. My landings had been poor and several times, my instructors had taken the control back.

"Well, this is it," I thought. "Today you'd better become a pilot. It's a lot more glamorous than becoming a corpse."

The take-off was fine. I made a big circle and went over the landing routine in my mind several times before heading in. I came in too high -- that was a whole lot safer than too low and one could always abort. I did.

I could see my instructor hollering at me on the ground. The next time would be it. It was. The landing wasn't perfect, but damn close to it. I got to the end of the runway, turned around, went back to the other end and took off again. And landed again.

All tolled, I took off and landed six times. I had soloed and survived -- six times. After the last one, I taxied over to my instructor. He said nothing. He climbed up onto the wing and into the second seat. I took off and flew us home. I had become a pilot.

That day was and still is the single most defining day of my life.

From Jackson, Tenn. (Primary Flight Training):

Saturday, August 7, 1943

Dear Folks,

Received your letter while I was still at Maxwell and sure was glad to hear from you. Fred has been telling me a little about the farm in his letter and I guess it's really coming along fine. I don't imagine I'll get much of a chance to see it this year as they sure don't give out any furloughs in our part of the Air Corps. We arrived here July 29 and have really been kept going ever since. We get up at 5:15 a.m. and don't stop until 7 p.m. and then we've got a good bit of homework to do so I don't get much of a chance to write except to Margie.

We fly every day and I love it. You can't realize just what it's like until you had a little time in the air. However, it is a darn tough job to learn as the army wants everything just so and it keeps a fellow thinking every minute of the time he's up there. The big thing now is to catch on fast and that seems to be the where the most of the fellows lose out. I'm trying like the devil and trusting to fate I make the grade. I have a very good instructor and in my opinion, that's half of it. We have ground school two hours a day, one hour on the Theory of Flight and one hour on Airplane Engines. So far I'm making out all right. We are flying Stearman Bi-Planes which are 220 horse power and are really nice ships. They are pretty fast and can really climb nice. We don't fly tomorrow, but we aren't allowed off the post and there is nothing here to do so we usually go up to the athletic area and fool around.

Well, folks, it's getting around to taps, so I guess I'd better cut this a little short. Drop me a line when you get time and let me know how everybody is.

As Ever,

Harry

From Primary Flight Training:

Wednesday, September 15, 1943

Dear Walt and Mary,

Well, folks, how's everything going back on the farm? I imagine by this time the biggest part of the work's about done. We were supposed to have open post tonight, but they took it away from us and consequently, I have to stay in. Margie got down last Saturday morning and needless to say, I was sure glad to see her and have her down with me to stay.

The flying seems to be coming along O.K. I now have 53 hours to my credit in the air and lately have started on acrobatics. They're a lot of fun, but a lot of work too and after flying for four hours, you don't feel too frisky. I still have one more check and then my acceptance ride and if I get through them all right, I'll be set. In the Air Corps, you just seem to live from one check ride to the next. So far, I've been pretty lucky and have had good days on my checks and if the old luck holds up, I'll get through.

Margie said you took the Plymouth off of her hands. If you have any trouble with the battery, don't be afraid to crank it as it is the easiest car to crank that I have ever come across. Fred was down the other week and I sure was glad to see him. We will finish up here around the end of the month and then will be sent to Basic. I don't [know] just where we will go but imagine it will be some place in Arkansas.

Well, it seems I'm about out of news so I'll close now. Drop me a line when you get the time and let me know how you are.

As Ever,

Harry

Tuesday, November 2, 1943

Hello Folks,

Just a few lines to let you know everything is coming along all right. Am really starting to get a little bit of time in these ships and hope to get in about four hours a day from now on. I will take my first solo cross country in this ship tomorrow and it should be quite an experience. Flying is quite a bit different than ground traveling as you have wind to reckon with and if you don't keep on your toes, you can be several miles off course before you realize it. However, when you figure this ship cruises at one hundred and thirty miles an hour and if you have a tail wind of twenty miles an hour, you are making good a ground speed of 150 mph you can really get around in a hurry.

We also start night flying tomorrow and that too should be quite an experience. We were scheduled to start last night but flying was called off as the weather was pretty bad. I have been very fortunate in regards to instructors as I have a swell one. He is just a young fellow as a matter of fact, he is younger than I am, but he sure knows his business.

I don't know whether I have told you or not but we are getting Link Trainer instruction too. I got ten hours at Primary, six hours here, and will get four more here. It is very interesting as it is practically the same as instrument flying and when you realize it costs thirty dollars an hour in civilian life it makes a fellow realize just how thorough the Army is in its training program.

Well, so much for the flying, as you know Margie is with me now and it is working out swell. She and two other Cadet wives have a small house and she has been nursing at the local hospital and that's a big help financially and it also gives her something to do and keeps her mind occupied. That seems to be the biggest problems with cadet wives - they have too much time on their hands. Well folks, I think I'll get around to closing now. Take care of yourselves and drop me a line when you get time.

As Ever

Harry

Newport, Ark.; from my mother, Margie, to Walt and Mary:

Mon., Nov. 8, 1943

Dear Folks,

This will be just a short note to let you know we are OK. I go to work again tomorrow on a private surgical case. I want to save as much this month as I can toward a 3-day pass which we will spend either in St. Louis, Little Rock, or the Ozark Mts. I would prefer the mts.

I earned $91 last month and I have about $15 of it left and Harry gave me $20 which I don't want to break. I have it hidden in my wallet.

They made it optional that the boys become Aviation Students and receive [dependent] allotments and now they changed them back to cadets and let them have allotments. I should be getting that soon.

Short interruption while we ate supper. We had 2 lamb chops apiece, peas, potatoes, cucumbers, lettuce and tomatoes, and spring onions. Not bad - eh?

Another interruption. Harry just called. He has 31 hrs. in the air here at this post. Today he flew at 8000 ft. and above a heavy bank of clouds with occasional breaks through which you could see the earth. He said it just took his breath away. Down here on the ground it was hazy and up there the sun was so bright he had to wear sunglasses.

I hope that on his leave in Feb. that he can take me up for a ride. I am anxious to fly with him.

My brother, Ray, has asked for a transfer to the Cadets. I hope he is accepted.

I received a V-letter from Franklin. He is in Sicily now and he has something to do with a show. He says its quite an interesting change.

Well, I must close. I'm sending a snapshot of Harry D. (as he is know in the army).

Love to all,

Margaret

Southeast Army Air Forces Training Center, Newport, Arkansas:

Friday, November 19, 1943

Dear Walt and Mary,

Well folks, here it is about the end of November and everything is still coming along all right. I have entered into several new phases of flying since I wrote you last. First, we started cross country flying and it is quite interesting. To date, we have made three solo cross country flights and the last two being about two hundred and fifty miles round trip. Air navigation is a subject within itself and it's not very hard to get lost. We then started night flying which is about the most difficult to get the hang of. I have seven hours of solo night flying and have made a total of thirty-two solo night landings of which eleven were blackout landings (no lights of any type used) however they weren't as hard as I thought they were going to be, not much different from daytime except you have to check everything a little closer. Two days ago, we started formation flying which is what will be used all of the time in combat. We will get quite a bit of formation flying at Advanced and there we will also start night formation flying which I imagine will be rather hard especially at first.

I now have fifty three hours in Basic Trainers of which twenty are dual and thirty-three solo. We should be finished here in about two more weeks and I have applied for Twin Engine Advanced School and feel fairly sure I will get it. We get ten hours instrument flying here and to date, I have six. It is quite different to fly instruments and I have been having quite a time getting into it, but everybody seems to be having the same trouble so it doesn't bother me too much. The ability to fly instruments is just about the best life insurance a pilot can have and the army is stressing it quite a bit more now than they ever did before.

We Cadets going through now are really getting several advantages as they have altered our flying instructions to conform to actual combat necessities. Our class has made a very good safety record and while we have had a few accidents, in general we have done pretty good. A room mate of mine was killed the other night in a mid-air collision and it sure was too bad. He was married on a Saturday night and killed the following Monday.

Well, so much for the flying. Margie is fine and has been working quite a bit at the local hospital and likes it very much. I have been able to spend most every weekend with her so far, but this week we fly Saturday afternoon, Sunday morning, and Sunday night. I go on my solo night cross country to Memphis, Little Rock and back home. I have received two letters from Beck* within the last week and everything seems the same with her. Fred wrote me from California and he sure had some trip.

I seem to be about out of news so I guess I'll get around to closing. Take care of yourselves and drop me a line and let me know how everything is back home.

Love,

Harry

P.S. Enclosed is a picture I had taken at Primary.

*Beck was my father's sister, an Army nurse stationed in Burma.

Southeast Army Air Forces Training Center Newport, Arkansas:

Thursday, December 2, 1943

Dear Walt and Mary,

Received your letter and was sure glad to hear from you. I imagine by the time Walter is well on the road to recovery* and is finding out it's no fun just to sit around with nothing to do. He and I sure differed on our methods of coming out of ether. I use to embarrass everybody in the room with my spectacular vocabulary. I'll never forget when I was about twelve and had my tonsils out. I laid there and would really tell everybody what I thought. Then I would look up at Mother, say, pardon me, and start right in again.

I imagine the old homestead doesn't seem the same since the plumbers have been there. I sure am glad you folks got around to it as it gets pretty cold in the winter if you know what I mean. I have received several letters from Beck lately and she seems to be coming along all right. Fred wrote me from the coast and he really must have had some trip.

I can tell you there is really no method of travel that can compare to plane. On my cross country hops, I often look down over the wing of my plane and watch a bus or car crawling along and almost pity them. Once flying gets in your blood, it's there to stay. I can hardly wait until the day I am able to take you folks up and show you around the sky.

We have finished our ground school here and only one more day of flying. I am going to twin engine advanced school at Stuttgart, Ark. and it suits me to a tee. We should be shipping [out] either Sunday or Monday and that will be my last phase of Cadet training. When I finish my two months there and everything goes all right, I'll get my wings. I am looking forward to getting a furlough then but don't have the slightest idea whether I will or not. I have had all of my check rides and passed them so I feel pretty good about that.

We had our graduation dance last night and it was a pretty nice affair. They had the post orchestra, all the coke and beer you could drink, and I thoroughly enjoyed myself. We left about midnight and I sure had a hard time dragging myself out of bed this morning. That's one thing the army hasn't been able to change, I still love my sleep.

Well folks, I guess I'll get around to closing now. Take care of yourselves and drop me a line and let me know how you're coming along.

Love,

Harry

P.S. My title is now A/C instead of A/S. Congress passed a law granting dependent allotments to cadets so I changed back.

Walter had obviously undergone some surgery. It was relatively minor. A/C means Aviation Cadet. A/S means Aviation Student.

From Stuttgart Army Air Field, Stuttgart, Arkansas:

Friday, January 7, 1944

Dear Walt and Mary,

Received your letter folks and was very glad to hear from you. Was sorry I couldn't be with you over the holidays but hope to see you before too long. We will more than likely graduate sometime in February and am really looking forward to a little furlough which will more than likely be ten days total time which will give me five or six days at home. It sure will be great to see the home town again and everybody back there. I hope by this time next Christmas, we can all be together again and maybe we can if some of the boys back home realize that seven cents an hour isn't the most important thing in the world. [Comment directed at steelworkers who were on or threatening to strike.]

Was glad to hear Walter is coming along all right and imagine he'll be back to normal in a few weeks. I'm glad everything on the farm is coming along O.K. Keep on raising plenty of pigs as we went on Jamison rations the first of the year and the food is really worth writing home about and stuffed pork chops really make a super meal. Our schedule here is fairly tight and lately have been getting quite a bit of flying in and that really gives a fellow an appetite. Most people think flying is a game, but in reality there is quite a bit of work attached to it and you're really ready for bed when the time comes. I believe I have told you that I am flying twin engine planes now and like them very much. I soloed this ship when I had six hours in it and at the present time have around twenty-three hours pilot and ten or twelve hours co-pilot. We get quite a bit of instrument flying here and will start cross country formation and night flying in about ten days or two weeks. I was on a cross country flight the other day and got down to Texas. We flew over the city of Texarkana which is on the border of Texas and Arkansas. It was around four hundred miles round trip and we made it in two and one half hours. I started flying radio beams today and really got a kick out of it. Beam flying is one of the most fascinating things I have come across in my Cadet career. My instructor is very good and seems to have a way of presenting things that makes even the complicated seem understandable. I don't imagine we will fly tomorrow as it has just started to snow and it is supposed to keep up for a couple of days.

Fred wrote me and told me all about his engagement and I sure am glad he got a girl who is as nice as she seems to be.

Margie is fine and sends her love. At the present time, she is working at the local hospital and likes it very much. The people down here are very nice and do everything to make us feel at home. Well, I guess I am about out of news so I guess I'll get around to closing. Tell Richard to drop me another line as I sure got a kick out of his letter.

Love

Harry

Your mother came down to the South to live with me during my post-Primary training. I don't think she trusted me on my own with all those pretty Southern belles running around. Anyway, that was really great. Having her join me made things much better. And since she was a nurse, she was able to find work at local hospitals everywhere we went. She could earn as much as $30 a day when I was earning $30 a month -- and she didn't let me forget it.

"I kept him in a fashion to which he had never been accustomed." my mother chimed in.

And she did too! We didn't want for anything.

I did well at twin engine training and really loved instrument flying. It was an academic exercise in the air.

Stuttgart, Arkansas; from my mother:

> Sun., Jan 16, 1944
>
> Dear Mary and Walt,
>
> I guess it is about time I should write. I have been very busy here in Stuttgart. I went to work the Sunday before Christmas and I've been working ever since with only time off duty when Harry is in town. Arkansas is certainly shy on nurses and Dr's., more so than Penna.
>
> Thank you very much for the Christmas money. Harry and I pooled it with our cash on hand and we intend to use it for his officers uniform. He bought a "Flight" hat last evening and he is going to buy a pair of pilot's wings this week. The odds and ends really count up so you know the gift was really appreciated.
>
> We had a very nice X-mas Eve and Christmas Day. X-mas eve we sat in the living room and talked of past Eve's and also sang carols & "We Three Kings Of Orient Are." Really made ourselves homesick.

We had Christmas dinner with the landlady and her family and 3 other cadets and their wives.

We got a lot of cards and we had a little tree and I had filled a stocking for Harry and had lots of fun watching him open the little things I got for him.

Harry gave me a nurse's watch. I've needed one badly and wouldn't buy it. So he picked it out and I bought it the next day. It is quite dainty and a lovely watch.

Rumor has it that they are to be commissioned on the 8th of Feb. so we expect to be home shortly after that date. We are both terribly anxious to get home and see everyone.

Were you surprised at the engagement? Fred wrote us in the beginning of Dec. and told us not to breathe a word. He wanted it to be a surprise. I think Helen is a lovely girl and I know they will be happy. We were both quite surprised and pleased.

You know, Mary, we were very happy at home, but too sure of ourselves for a while. Since we have had to be separated for a while it makes a big difference in one's outlook on life and happiness. I certainly appreciate Harry and the home he provided for me a whole lot more now. He is so sweet – sweeter every time I see him (which is just once a week). If only he comes through this OK. I was able to send him off last Feb with a smile. I'm afraid I won't be able to do that when he goes overseas.

I have to laugh at him. He says, "Just imagine, Margie! Your husband can fly a plane, and a big one at that!"

He is amazed at himself and just thrilled to pieces about having been able to come through cadet training.

You should see our scrap book. Harry is so proud of it. He has read it several times. I'm so glad I decided to make one for him as he likes to read it and it reminds him of things he had already started to forget.

I hope you had a nice Christmas. The thing we missed most about the holidays was X-mas Eve at the Carlins with the family.

Do you remember that we announced our engagement 5 years ago on X-mas Eve at your home?

Stuttgart is quite a nice little town. I like it quite a bit. But the country is so flat and the weather is very peculiar. Dr. Drennen says it should be called "the funny South" not "the sunny South." Of course, I feel we are more West than South but they claim to be Southerners.

I plan to quit working about the first of the month so that I can visit Harry at the post and be in on all the latest rumors that run rampant the last week or so. I just can't miss anything. And too, I want to send most of things – uniforms, etc. – home ahead of us and then we won't have much to bother us on the train. Just Harry's things. We expect to come home by Pullman car. I had a berth when I came down, but this will be Harry's first experience in a sleeper. I don't expect to sleep much as the whole train will be new officers & friends so we will probably have a high old time coming home.

Well, I am going to try to write to French & Laura tonight too, so I'll say Goodnight. We'll see you (y'all) soon.

Love,

Margaret

Finally, after I got my wings in February, we had a leave and went home. That leave was the first time I had been home in a year.

The next step was training on the planes we would fly in combat. We were sent to Columbia, South Carolina. We were made up into crews and started flying B-25's.

The B-25's were known as Mitchells and were made by North American. They were great planes -- powerful, sturdy, and a dream to fly. I took to them very well. Bombers were well-suited to my methodical approach and the B-25's were, in my opinion, the best of them.

The B-25's were medium bombers. They carried about half the load of the B-17's and 24's and had a range of about 1500 miles round trip. But they were versatile. They could be outfitted for strafing and to provide heavy-duty ground support with four 50-caliber machine guns and one 75mm cannon in a solid nose and a package of four 50-caliber machine guns on the side of the cockpit, or for bombing with a glass nose for the navigator/bombardier. The bombers had a capacity of 5000 pounds. They also had one fixed 50-Caliber machine gun in the nose and one hand-held 50 for the bombardier. All versions had a top turret with two 50-caliber machine guns and another set of twin 50's in the tail. The 25's were used extensively in both roles, bombers and strafers – and, of course, on Doolittle's raid on Tokyo.

B-25's were an easily identifiable airplane with two engines and twin rudders on a boom at the tail. There were seven variations of the B-25. The A, B, C, and D models were bombers and primarily saw service in the earlier part of the war. The G, H, models were the strafers and ground-support models. The J's were bombers and incorporated all of the improvements made in the other models. They were used in the latter part of the war - when I was overseas.

Regardless, the B-25's were great planes to fly. They took a lot of punishment and still kept flying. They could fly on one engine if necessary and could handle a belly landing and still remain intact.

Columbia, South Carolina - after the furlough home:

> Friday, February 25, 1944
>
> Dear Walt and Mary,
>
> Thought I'd better drop you a few lines and let you know we received the money all right. Sure do appreciate it a lot as contrary to my expectations we may not get paid for a couple of weeks. South Carolina is much nicer than I thought it was going

to be. It is now spring down here and we go around in short sleeves during the day but wear a blouse at night. Second Lt.'s are a dime a dozen here but they do treat us much nicer than when we were cadets. We eat at the Officers Club and the food is pretty good. You always have a choice of two meats and plenty to go along with it. Margie was out for supper tonight and I imagine she will eat out on the post quite a bit as it only costs about half as much as it does in town and if anything the food is better.

We have a very nice set up here. I am allowed to live off the post and don't have to maintain a room in the B.O.Q. I have to report on the post every morning at eight thirty and can leave at five p.m. At the present time, I am attached to the Replacement Depot and do not do any flying. I expect to be transferred in a couple of weeks to the flying part of the field or be transferred to another field somewhere near here. At the present time, we have a couple of classes a day in camouflage, chemical warfare and code. We also underwent another physical examination and are being give our shots over as it has been almost a year since we had them. Man, they really gave my left arm a work out! The first day my arm absorbed typhoid, tetanus, cholera, small pox, and another one that I can't remember. I really had myself a beautiful limb for a couple of days. I sure wish they would find a more pleasant method of making one immune to everything they think you might get.

I guess by this time, Fred and Helen are happily married and are enjoying their little trip to the mountains. I sure think he got himself a darn nice girl and think he'll be a lot happier now that he has a home of his own.

I believe I'd better get around to closing now as it is getting a little late and I want to get up around six thirty in the morning. Take care of yourself and drop us a line when you can.

Love,

Harry and Margie

Columbia, South Carolina:

Sunday, March, 19 1944

Dear Walt and Mary,

Well folks, here it is Sunday again and as this is our day off, I thought I'd drop you a few lines to let you know everything is still coming along all right. I was transferred from the Replacement Depot to the 309th Bombardment Group early last week and like our new set up quite a bit. I will more than likely be a co-pilot on a B-25J which is the latest model of the B-25 series. As yet, I still haven't been up in one of these planes, but I report to the flight line tomorrow morning at seven thirty and expect to start flying some time next week. I do not know whether I will receive any transition training or just be assigned to a crew and get the hang of this plane from the first pilot. They've got more pilots down here than I ever knew existed in the whole Air Corps and quite a large percentage of them are men back from combat who have been to a rest camp, had their furlough, and are now ready to go over again. I sure hope I tie up with someone like this as I imagine I'll be able to pick up quite a few tricks of the trade. One thing I have been able to find out is that if we are sent to the European Theatre of Operations, we will fly our own planes over. Who would have ever thought a couple of years ago that I'd ever fly the ocean? I imagine it will be quite an experience and am really looking forward to it.

Margie and I have moved downstairs in the house we are staying at and have a very nice room. There is a fire place in it and I never realized just how nice one of them was. We have found a swell cafeteria up town so all in all, we have a darn nice set up. The town of Columbia is very nice and I sure am glad I was sent here. It is by far the nicest I have seen in the south and the stores are very good. I bought a rain coat last night and it sure is a beauty.

Last night, we went to see the stage play "Junior Miss" and it was very good. The actors were local amateurs, but is was as good acting as I have ever seen. Last Sunday we saw the movie

"A Guy Named Joe" and when it comes to Coatesville, be sure and see it as it is the best picture of the Air Corps that I have ever seen. Also the bombers that Spencer Tracy flies in the beginning of the picture are the ones that I fly and also the picture was filmed for the most part at the field here.

Well, folks, I guess I'll get around to closing. I'll send you the money in a little while as everything is just about straightened out. I received a letter from Beck dated March 1, but she doesn't have anything new to report. Take care of yourselves and drop us a line when you get time.

Love,

Harry and Margie

P.S. Understood the income tax instructions all right and sent the forms in, using Box 727 as the return address so all we have to do now is wait. Thanks an awful lot for the trouble as I would not have know where to start to begin to fill out one of those forms.

Some things truly never do change!

I liked the guys in my crew -- Ferrell Holley, Joe Semanak, Carl Coombs, Donald Dick, and Jim Cordell. Holley's and Semanak's wives had also joined them. We saw each other socially a lot. We became a crew.

The only incident occurred on one test flight from Oklahoma back to South Carolina. Each plane flew alone leaving Oklahoma at set intervals to test the navigator's skills. Joe was the navigator / bombardier and knew his business but on this flight, he didn't do well. If you make on mistake in your calculations early on, that mistake will just compound itself for the rest of the flight. That apparently happened to Joe because he missed the whole state of South Carolina. I could understand missing the base or missing Columbia, but not missing the whole goddamned state, even if it is small!

It was getting dark and there were no familiar landmarks in sight. We took the plane down and located some railroad tracks. We started following them on the assumption that they would lead to a town and to an airstrip. They did and we got back to our base -- two hours late. We landed and ran out of gas on the runway just after touching down. We couldn't even taxi off the runway! No one said anything. No one had to.

Margie and the other wives had been summoned to the base because of our lateness. They were quite relieved when we got in.

We received our overseas orders in Columbia, South Carolina, but were to go to Savannah, Georgia first. Our wives were not to accompany us, but Betty Semanak drove Margie and Becky Holley to Savannah for one last visit before we went overseas...and, boy, did we 'visit'! That was May, 3rd.

Saying good-bye was hard. We didn't know if we would ever see each other again. The War was starting to sink in. After three days in Savannah – there was some delay with the plane -- we were shipped overseas.

Chapter Four
Heading Overseas

Hunter Field, Savannah, Georgia:

Wednesday, May 3, 1944

Dear Margie,

Well, honey, it is now eight p.m. and we are still here. We didn't get our plane today, but imagine we will tomorrow morning. I slept all afternoon kind of resting up and the sack sure felt good. However, I'll have to get used to solo sack time all over again. I signed the will today and they will mail it to you, as a matter of fact, you will probably get it before this letter arrives, the power of attorney will also be mailed to you.

I sure did hate to see you go, dear. I love you so much and it was heaven having you with me. However, time still slips by pretty fast and then we can be together again for good. Honey, you take good care of yourself and don't work too hard. Try not to take your job too seriously and let it get you down. Think about me a lot, dear, only try not to worry. I'll come through all right, a good deal of it is knowing your business and, honey, I can handle my end of it and the rest of the crew are all very capable. You can be (and so can I) very thankful that I got on the crew I did. It's just about as good as they come.

I'm going to try and write you every day and if you don't hear from me, it will be because we are moving. You can write me at the return address on this letter and I will get the mail. My foot locker will more than likely come through in a couple of days and I will have to send it C.O.D. so it's not because I don't have the money. I hope you girls have a nice trip home and I'm awfully glad you're going with Betty. It is much better than traveling alone and you'll be company for each other.

You don't have to worry about sending me any razor blades, dear, as I got a box of one hundred Gillette blades today and that will last me over a year and, little girl, I expect to be back in this country by them. Well, dear, I am going to get around to closing now. Take care of yourself and always remember, dear, I love you more than anything in the world.

Your Loving Husband,

Harry

May 4 - no letter; received plane; test flight.

Friday, May 5, 1944

Dearest Margie,

Well, honey, another day has passed and we are still here. We are all packed to leave, but have been held up a little due to some trouble with the plane. I feel sure that we will be gone tomorrow. I received your letter from S.C. today, dearest, and I sure was glad to hear from you and know that everything was coming along all right.

At the present time, I am trying to call you on the phone but have been unsuccessful so far. The call got through to both Olie's and French's but no one answered. I do not know just where you are but thought I would try and get a call through as I believe this will be my last chance to call you. Beginning with my next stop, all of my mail will be censored and I believe I will have my A.P.O. number.

We were up in our ship yesterday and it sure is swell. I flew it quite a bit and really liked the way it handled. I think it is all right for me to tell you that we will fly where we are going to and, now mind you, keep this to yourself, and I'm not even sure that I will be able to or not, but I will try to look up Ray E. on our way. I have not been told where we are going or by what route but that is all for the better as I would rather get there safely than know too much about it. What I mentioned above is just the conclusion I've drawn and please dearest don't repeat it.

Holley and I are writing here in the mess hall office while we are waiting for our phone calls. Joe has put through a call and at the present time is eating hard boiled eggs and playing the slot machines. The weather down here has been fairly warm in the day time, but it gets pretty cool at night. The mosquitoes seem to be having a field day and you can't stay outside too long. We had a little free time this afternoon, so we all hit the sack. No sooner had I dropped off to sleep that I started to dream about you. I woke up just in time and thought now isn't that something. It was a piperoo and then I dropped back to sleep and started dreaming about you again. I woke up just in time again and, honey, you were just as sweet as ever. Dear, I love you more than anything in the whole world and to me you're all a girl could ever be. You're awfully sweet, dear, and I wouldn't trade you for a million others.

Well, dearest, I must close now. Please take care of yourself and remember, honey, I'll always be all yours. I love you very much, dear.

Your Loving Husband,

Harry

We got our overseas orders once we were in the plane, and were told not to open them until we were airborne. We opened them immediately. We went to Lakeland, Florida, San Juan, Puerto Rico, Georgetown, British Guyana, Belem and Natal, Brazil, Ascension Island, Liberia, Marrakech, Morocco, and then finally to Algiers. Each of the legs of the journey was roughly an eight-hour flight. It was my first time outside the U.S.

As you will note from the letters written on the way overseas, discussions of precise locations were prohibited.

May 6 - no letter; believe started overseas; first stop - Florida.
May 7 - location uncertain: probably Puerto Rico.

Sunday, May 7, 1944

Dearest Margie,

Well, honey, here it is Sunday evening and I thought I'd better drop my honey a few lines. We have moved again, so I guess we are really on our way. Didn't have much to do last night so we took in a show. I guess we'll take one in again tonight. I received your letter yesterday, dear, and I sure was glad to hear from you. Receiving a letter from you, dearest, is just about the nicest think I know. Everything is coming along fine and I am feeling fine and in good health.

Starting with this letter, dear, all of my mail will be censored and as this is all new to me, you'll have to bear with me for a while. Semenak and another navigator are having a discussion on navigation and I'm having a devil of a time trying to concentrate on this letter. While I happen to think of it, dear, my watch stopped. I am supposed to be issued one here and I am going to try and send this one home, however, I do not know whether I will be able to or not. I don't know what is the matter with it.

I flew a couple of hours today and imagine I will be doing more as time goes on because it relieves Holley and gives me practice which I guess I can't get too much of. Well, dearest, I think I'll sign off now and will try to a few more lines a little later when things quiet down a bit.

Well, dear - here I am back again. It is now about 11 p.m. We went to the show and saw Andy Hardy's *Blond Trouble* and I enjoyed it quite a bit. Then we went to the Officer's Club and had a few drinks. It is very quiet now and I've been thinking of you an awful lot. I don't know whether I have told you lately or not dear, but honey, you're the prettiest and sweetest little girl I have ever seen. Take care of yourself, honey, and remember I'm all yours and I love you very much. I guess I'd better get around to closing now and hit the sack and do a little dreaming about my honey. Good night, dear, and don't forget to write every day.

Your Loving Husband,

Harry

Monday, May 8, 1944

Dearest Margie,

I am now in the Officers Club and it is time drop my honey a few lines. Nothing new or exciting happened today. I finally got a watch issued to me and it is really nice. It is an Elgin make and I am very well pleased with it. While I happen to think of it dear, the A.P.O. number that I am using will not be permanent, but mail will reach me if you use it. When I arrive at my final destination, I will have one with only three numbers to it.

I imagine by this time, honey, you are home and fairly well settled. Give everyone my regards and tell the folks I was asking for them. If you happen to see Aunt Mary, tell her I will drop her a line as soon as I get settled. While I happen to think of it, dearest, I increased my class "E" allotment to the bank. They figured up how much I will make overseas and I had way too much money, so I increased the allotment to $175 per month. That should give us a nice little amount by the time the war is over so maybe we can build the little home we've always wanted or maybe to put it towards a small farm. Try not to use the money unless you need it as it will be a big help when we try to settle down again.

Well, dearest, I guess that's about all that's new today and there's not much more I can write except to tell you again how much I love you. It's an awful lot, dear, and I'll always be all yours and you keep your love all for me. Good night, Honey, take good care of yourself and remember I love you very, very much.

Your Loving Husband

Harry

P.S. Enclosed is the allotment change. Keep a copy and give one to the bank. The increase is effective July 1 and the original June 1.

P.S.2 The forms are not in my possession now so I'll send them later.

Love,

Harry

New Location - probably Georgetown, British Guyana.

Tuesday, May 9, 1944

Dearest Margie,

Well, Honey, it is now about quarter of eight and about time for me to drop my honey a few lines. We just got back from the Officers Club and it s is very nice. Everything is coming along fine and we are making out very well. I sure will be glad when I start receiving mail as your letters mean so very much to me, however, I will try and write you every day as I know you are doing the same. I can hardly realize that I won't to be able to see you or Beck or Fred for quite a while, but such are the misfortunes of war.

I hope you are well, dearest, and are coming along all right. I love you, honey, very much, dear, and miss you an awful lot. I haven't mailed my watch back yet and if I can't get it cleaned, I will send it to you. There is nothing new to report that I am allowed to write, so I guess I kind of cut this a little short. Take care of yourself and remember you are all mine.

Your Loving Husband,

Harry

Location uncertain; probably Georgetown, British Guyana.

Wednesday, May 10, 1944

Dearest Margie,

Well, honey, here's the daily letter to my little wife and, honey, it's so hot I can hardly keep the sweat from marring the paper. Everything is still coming along fine and I am feeling all right. While I happen to think of it, dearest, I am about two thirds through the book "The Robe" and it is by far the most fascinating book I have ever read. I pick it up every opportunity that I get and will surely hate to finish it. There is nothing new to report and even if there were, I wouldn't be able to tell you; however, when I am permanently stationed, I believe it will be a lot better and I'll be able to tell you some of the experiences I have had.

Holley and Joe are both fine and send their regards. The rest of the boys are fine and I sure am glad I am in the crew I am. Every one seems to know their job and that is very important. Well, dear, I know this letter is awful short, but there is not much I can write about. I love you and awful lot, honey, and want you to know that I'm all yours and always will be. Take care of yourself and be sure to write me everyday.

Love you,

Your Loving Husband,

Harry

Location uncertain; probably Georgetown, British Guyana.

Thursday, May 11, 1944

Dearest Margie,

Another day has passed and I am now starting a letter to the sweetest little wife in the whole world. I am now in the Officers Club and Joe and Holley are back preparing for the sack. I sure do not go for this solo sack time and find it quite hard to get used to it. I guess having you with me for the past year sort of spoiled me, but, honey, it sure was worth it. It was heaven being with you all of that time and I guess we both should be very thankful that we had all of that time together. I don't believe that either one of us quite appreciated each other until we had been separated for a while, but I sure know now how much you mean to me and I know that I mean just as much to you.

I sure will be glad when your mail starts coming through. It is rather difficult for me to write under these circumstances. We will be able to talk things over even if it is just in a letter. We can start making plans again. I can hardly wait, dear, until we can have our own little home again and this time there will be quite a few little co-pilots running around the place. I don't believe you ever realized just how much I wanted children but I thought we should be a little more on our feet before we had them. I felt this war was coming a long time ago and knew I had a part of play in it, not a big part, maybe, but contributing my share small though it may be. Whether or not I was right remains to be seen, but, dearest, I do want you to know how much I love you and that I want only you to bear my (pardon, I mean our) children. Don't lose hope, dearest, time will pass quickly and we'll be back together again before we realize.

Goodnight, honey. I am going to close now . Take care of yourself and remember, honey, I am all your and love you very much.

Your Loving Husband,

Harry

Belem, Brazil

Friday, May 12, 1944

Dearest Margie,

Well, honey, another day has passed and we are now in Brazil. Kind of surprised that I am able to tell you where I am at the present, aren't you? Well, dear, you are no more amazed that I am, but when we arrived here, we were told that we could say that we were in Brazil. We flew over the Amazon River and it is quite a huge river. Over seventy miles wide at the mouth and I would sure hate to cross it using the old Water Witch* for power. It is quite muddy in color and was very distinctive from the air. I also crossed the equator and can now say I have been in the southern hemisphere.

* *Water Witch was a brand of outboard motor in the 2-3 h.p. range.*

We are having quite a time with the natives, they don't know what we're talking about and vice versa. One has to leave the States to realize just how far advanced of the rest of the world we Americans are. The food has been fairly good so far and if it doesn't get much worse I won't have too much room to kick. Flying down here has been a wonderful experience and I have really learnt a lot. Holley has let me do quite a bit of the flying and I've sure enjoyed it and put it all to good use.

We had native oranges and bananas for supper and they are quite different from what we have back home. They are both pure green on the outside and the oranges are seedless (at least they seemed to be), they use a sharp knife and cut the skin off and then slice them down, not eating the center. The bananas have a funny taste and I did not care for them too much. What amazed me most was the coffee. They do not drink it at all like we do. It is very bitter and very strong and they only fill the cup half full and add nothing to it at all. That is one custom I am altering to suit my own taste, but even with the decorations, it can't come up to good old American coffee. Whiskey is very plentiful down here at the officers clubs and that surprised me very much as it is such brands as Canadian Club, etc., however, it does a lot more good here than back in the States as a drink or two in the evening sure breaks it up.

I haven't had a chance to write to any of the folks except you dear, but after I get settled at my final destination, I'll let them know how things are coming along. The weather here is just as you would expect it to be in the tropics, very hot and an awful lot of moisture in the air and during the day, you have to take it easy except of course when you're flying as it is cooler upstairs. I ran into a little item in the Px tonight and bought you a little present that I thought you'd like. Be sure and let me know if you receive it and how you like my selection. Cigarettes here are only a nickel a pack and seem plentiful, so that makes it OK. By this time, I am a confirmed Chesterfield smoker for what reason I do not know except that now they seem to taste better so I've been smoking them.

Well, dearest, I guess I'd better get around to closing now. Take care of yourself and don't forget that I love you very much. I'll write again tomorrow, dear, and you be sure and get a letter off to me every day. Good night, honey, and don't worry too much about me. I'm feeling fine and coming along all right. Of course, I miss you an awful lot, but it won't be too long until we're together again.

Your Loving Husband,

Harry

No movement.

Saturday, May 13, 1944

Dearest Margie,

Well, honey, old gal, how's everything coming along today? Fine, I hope, dear. Things sure went fine for me today. First, I went down to the censor's office and mailed my little present to you, dear, and also my watch as this was the first chance I had to do it. I also mailed my letter to you plus a package of post cards. You will also find a foreign dollar that I thought you might like for our scrap book.

Enclosed in this letter is Brazilian note that is worth twenty five cents. We had a fairly easy day today and the rest sure did me good. We were able to get our clothes laundered here and the price was really amazing. For sixty-one cents, we had four uniforms washed and ironed plus three sets of underwear. I damn near popped over when I saw the irons that the native women use. They are quite large and instead of using electricity to supply the heat, the center of them is hollow and they fill them with hot charcoals and that heats the iron. When it gets too cool to iron with, they go outside to a little fire then get some more charcoals. Some set-up don't you think?

We are taking Adabian tablets daily and they are the most miserable tasting tablets in the world. They take the place of quinine for the suppression of malaria.

As I have said before, dearest, I sure will be glad when your mail starts coming through. I sure would like to have one of your letters now. You don't realize how much the mean to me, dear. I love you so very much and want you to know just how sweet you are. You're the nicest and prettiest little girl that there ever was and you've got a husband who thinks the world of you. Well, honey, I guess I'll get around to closing now. Take care of yourself and remember each day I'm away from you means that I'll be home just one day sooner.

All my love,

Your husband,

Harry

May 14 moved to Natal, Brazil.

Just before we were to head over the ocean from Natal, Brazil, I decided that it was time to say something to Joe. Ascension Island was an eight hour flight away and a very small target. There was little, if any, margin for error. As we were walking out to the plane, I said to Joe, "If you miss Ascension Island like you missed South Carolina, you aren't getting into the life raft. I will see to that."

Joe knew that I meant it. And I did. He hit Ascension Island dead on. He passed my test with flying colors and from that day on, he was more than OK with me.

May 15 moved to Ascension Island.

>Monday, May 15, 1944
>
>Dearest Margie,
>
>It is now about ten minutes to six and I'm going to start this letter before supper, but don't imagine I'll finish it until later this evening.
>
>We arrived here and I didn't have time to write yesterday, but am right back on the ball today.
>
>We got up around eight am and have had quite a day. This afternoon, we went fishing believe it or not, and I sure wish you could have been with me. We only had hand lines and meat for bait, but as the waves came in, you could see the fish in them. I don't know what the name of them was, but they were built like a sunfish, were black and about ten inches long. They had teeth in them like a horse. As soon as you would throw the line in, the water would be black with fish around the bait. I caught nine, the engineer seven, and the tail gunner three. We fished for about two hours and I sure would have liked to have had my casting rod and some plugs with me as it was a fisherman's paradise as far as getting bites was concerned. I have wanted to

go fishing for quite a while back and sure am glad that I got the chance as it was a lot of fun.

We are going to a show tonight and the theater is quite unique. There is a screen out in the open and you sit on the ground on the side of a little hill. There is always a breeze blowing here and it is lovely in the evening. Just one of the nights when a fellow would like to have his best girl (meaning you, honey, girl) beside him with his arm around her and just hold her real close and every now and then, she'd look up at him and he'd lean over and kiss her. We haven't been separated very long, dearest, but I'm just waiting for the day when we'll be back together again. I've got an awful lot of loving to catch up on and the sooner we can start, the better off we will be.

It is now after supper and I guess I'd better get around to continuing this letter to my sweet little wife. I'll be so very glad when I start to hear from you, dearest, but that time's coming and I sure an looking forward to it. When you write, be sure and tell me if you received my watch and the present your husband bought for you. I have been wondering what you have been doing with yourself, honey, whether you are back to work yet or you took a little vacation and got settled again.

Well, honey, this starts page three and I'm just about out of news. I want to thank you, honey, for addressing these letters, honey, it sure has made it a lot easier and it keeps reminding me what a thoughtful wife I have. You're swell, dear, and I love you very much.

Your Loving Husband,

Harry

Roberts Field, Liberia.

Tuesday, May 16, 1944

Dearest Margie,

Well, honey, here it is the 16th of May, your husband's birthday and he is spending it in the western part of Africa. I am allowed to tell you that much, but of course, I cannot disclose what part of Western Africa I am in at the present time. I am covered with mosquito repellent and stink like the devil. I am enclosing a few franc notes as these are used all over Africa and we are permitted to send them home. I got weighed today and hit the scale at 163, so you can see that I 'm not losing any weight and feel fine. It is very hot here and I can honestly say now that I love cold weather. I never appreciated snow before, but believe me, dear, I believe I could live in an igloo.

I read your birthday letter and, dear, it was very sweet. You don't know how much a letter like that means when I am away from you. I love you very much, dear, and miss you very much. I am writing in our barracks and the lighting is miserable and I can hardly see the paper.

The food so far has been much better than I had expected and the only complaint I might have would be that we have been rationed one pint of beer per day and, darling, I never knew how delicious beer could be. All of it has been first grade but one drink far from quenches a fellow's thirst. If any one back home even suggests prohibition, tell them to go jump in a lake! Well, dear, I guess I'll undress and climb through my mosquito netting and hit the sack. I am pretty tired and sure could use some sleep. I am going to close now. Take care of yourself and remember, honey, I love you very much.

All of my love,
Your Loving Husband,

Harry

Margie's Birthday Letter.

Tuesday, May 2, 1944
(To be opened May 16, 1944)

Dearest Harry,

First of all, Honey, I want to wish you a very happy birthday. I do hope you will have a nice time today and not work too hard.

Harry, I just don't know what to say to you as you will probably be very far away from me when you read this. But, above all, I want you to know that you are the dearest and best husband a girl ever had and I love you so terribly much.

I have already given you a couple of little gifts for your birthday, so I haven't anything else to give you. But I can send you my love - all of it and I can say that I'll be waiting for you and loving you more than ever. Do take care of yourself for me, dear. I just couldn't live without you.

Harry, I promise that I'll always belong just to you - even forever and ever. I'll never belong to anyone else. So - as I said in my letter to you last year – my main gift to you is me.

Honey, I love you more than anything in the world. So for your birthday - all my love and good wishes. Take good care of yourself.

Your loving wife,

Margie

Roberts Field, Liberia.

Wednesday, May 17, 1944
Somewhere in West Africa

Dearest Margie,

Well, honey girl, it is now quarter to two and Joe and I are sitting on our bunks writing to our wives. The barracks are very nice here, nothing fancy but still pretty nice. I am getting used to shaving with cold water and it is not as bad as one might expect. I just took a shower and really feel swell. There is a nice breeze blowing and it is very nice. In my last few letters, I have enclosed some [censored] money that is used all over Africa and I wonder if it has gone through all ready. Did you receive your stockings, honey? I hope so and be sure and tell me if you like them and how they fit. We sure have had a lot of wonderful experiences coming over and I sure do wish you could have been along to enjoy them. It has been an education in itself and Joe has turned out to be quite a capable navigator. I do half of the piloting and am doing all right even if I must say so myself. I am getting to like the plane more every day and am really glad I got assigned to this type.

I am very anxious to hear from you and how you are coming along and whether you are settled yet. Fred's deferment should be up pretty soon and I wonder if it will be renewed. Have you heard from Ray E. lately and if so, how is he getting along? I thought there for awhile I might get to see him, but I guess not now. I haven't seen a newspaper for about two weeks but I heard a big push had been started in Italy and I hope they get going and get the war over before too darn long. I am ready to come back to you now dear and the sooner the better. Well, honey, I am going to close now. Take care of yourself and remember, dear, you're all mine and I love an awful lot and think about you all of the time.

Your Loving Husband,

Harry

Roberts Field, *Liberia*.

> Thursday, May 18, 1944
> Somewhere in West Africa
>
> Dearest Margie,
>
> Well, honey, here it is Thursday and today am tired as a dog and do not expect to be long out of the sack. Everything is still about the same and coming along all right. I just got back from supper and despite the fact that I took a bath about an hour ago, I am so sleepy I can hardly keep my eyes open. Today, America seems very far away and I have been thinking of you constantly. In a way, you seem so close to me that it is hard to realize that we have been separated.
>
> From the way things are going in Italy now, it may not be too long before the Jerrys throw in the towel and if the Japs don't last too long, we will be able to be together again. What I wouldn't give to be able to hold you in my arms again and hear you whisper, "I love you, honey." I guess I need a good loving from you, dear.
>
> I am writing this in the Officer's Day Room and it is quite some place - a couple of wooden tables and some chairs thrown around. Things overseas are nothing like they were back in the states, but aren't really as bad as I had expected. The food at this place is about the same as the last and tonight, I drank my first powdered milk and it tastes like a cross between regular milk and canned milk and I imagine after you used to it that it will be OK.
>
> Well, honey, I am going to get around to closing. Do take care our lovely self and remember, dearest, I am all yours and love you very, very much and I think you're the sweetest little girl in the whole world.
>
> All of my love,
> Your Loving Husband,
>
> Harry

We found out during our layover in Brazil that the other planes had orders all the way to Corsica. Ours only went as far as Marrakech. When we got to Marrakech, we had a minor mechanical problem and there were no parts or mechanics. We didn't want to stay there with no parts and no mechanics, so we went to Algiers on our own.

When we got to Algiers, we checked with the Commanding Officer and were told to stay put. He had no record of our orders, no parts, and no idea of where to send us. The other planes went on to Corsica.

We stayed in Algiers for about three days until our orders and a replacement starter caught up with us.

May 20 - Algiers, Algeria.

> Saturday, May 20, 1944
>
> Dearest Margie,
>
> I am writing this letter in the plane and that is the reason for my using this stationary. It belongs to the radio operator and while we are waiting to have a starter installed I thought I would take advantage of the time and drop a few lines to my little wife.
>
> I am now in North Africa and it is quite a bit like home. The Mediterranean is very beautiful and there always seems to be breeze blowing. We were allowed in town last night and it was quite an experience. The town itself was fairly modernistic only dirty as the deuce. The streets were very narrow and quite dark. We went to a movie and all the talking was in French and I didn't know what was coming off. It was funny as the devil trying to follow the there of the story when you couldn't understand what the actors were saying. I had a couple of glasses of French wine and it isn't too bad at all. We ate at an American Officers Club and the food stunk. They don't seem to eat anything but stew over here and the food at the camp is very much better.

I expect to start receiving mail from you in a little while and you can't imagine how much I am looking forward to it. You mean so very much to me, honey, and not hearing from you has made me pretty lonely for you. However, when I begin to receive your mail it should really do the trick.

Everybody is fine and we are enjoying the trip quite a bit. It seems I have developed quite a bit more confidence not only in myself, but things in general. They seem to be making quite a bit of progress in Italy and I sure hope it continues.

Well dearest, I am going to close now. Take care of yourself, remember you're all mine and I'm all yours. So long, dear, and don't forget to write.

Your Loving Husband,

Harry

Still in Algiers, Algeria.

Sunday, May 21, 1944
Somewhere in North Africa

Dearest Margie,

Honey, I received my first letter from you this morning and I was never so glad to receive a bit of mail in my life. It was your letter of May 11 and that was the one that had the color photograph in it. Honey, I just sat and looked at your picture. You looked so very sweet and honey send me a photograph every now and then so I'll be able to see just how pretty you really are. You don't have to worry, dear, I'll be careful and before you know it, I'll be back with you. You said you hoped your letters were interesting to me, dear, of course they are. And as long as we're separated, I'll look forward each day for your letter so please don't even miss one day and write two if you have time. You don't know how hungry I was for mail.

I was glad to hear Ray E. got S/Sgt. and hope he goes right on up the line. Also, think that Don got a good deal and just hope that he makes the most of it. The camp that I am now at is really something. We are in tents, dirt floor, and no light facilities. The latrine is down across a field and we wash out of two water tanks that have a hose connection on it. I haven't had bath in three or four days and am now getting used to my own smell.

I guess I have read your letter five or six times and intend to reread it until I receive your next one. The food is still fairly good and we are now eating out of mess kits. I am sitting in our tent and using a gas mask box to write on and it isn't a half bad deal at all.

It gets quite hot here during the day, but cools off considerably at night. The countryside is fairly rugged and is rather pretty too.

Well, dear, I am going to close now. Take care of yourself, think a lot about me, remember I love you very much and, honey, I hope you are pregnant too. I was wrong in us not having a baby and this time I really hope and pray you are. By the time your receive this, you will more than likely know, so tell me if you are and don't be afraid to let me know.

Your Loving Husband,

Harry

Chapter Five
Ed and I - Reunion At Alesan

From Algiers, it was on to join the 340th Bomb Group on Corsica. This island in the Mediterranean between France and Italy had been transformed into a maze of landing strips, which from the air looked like brown arrows pointed at the heart of Germany. As we were coming in on the final approach, I saw the twisted wreckages of airplanes pushed off to the side of the field. Jerry had been there and really worked it over.

"Say, George, what the devil happened to this place?" Donald Dick, our gunner, asked.

"Looks like they had a little excitement all right," I replied. I then switched the control box from interphone to radio.

"Genora, Genora, Army 7735 number one on the final approach; over."

"Army 7735, this is Genora. You are clear to land; out."

As we parked our plane and crawled down through the hatch, we saw we had quite an audience of G.I.'s.

"How are the States?" was the first question we were asked.

"Oh, they're not worth a damn since we left," was Dick's reply.

Meanwhile I was looking around wondering what was coming next. The field surely was beat up and I was getting more curious by the minute. Suddenly a jeep pulled up along side of us.

"Hop in, fellows, and I'll take you over to Operations."

"O.K., boys," I said, "snap it up. It'll be dark before too long and I want to get a sack made up while it's still light."

At Operations we were assigned to the 487th Bomb Squadron and were told to wait around for a truck to take us to the squadron area.

"George, do you think they get bombed very often?"

"I don't know, Dick, but I'm sure glad we missed this one."

Coombs, our radio man, was talking over the female situation with another sergeant.

"You should have been with us in Algiers," I heard him say; "All you needed was a little money and, boy, you were set."

"How long since you left there?" the sergeant asked.

"Two days."

"I'd wait about a week before I felt too good about it if I were you."

"Oh, hell, she was a nice girl. Just needed some money. Seems her mother was sick and had to have an operation."

"Poor kid!"

"I like these foreign dames. They don't think they're so damn much, like they do back home."

"They aren't."

"How're the women here?"

"Brother, there hasn't been a nice one on this island since Napoleon left to conquer France."

"You don't know where to look for them."

This delightful conversation was interrupted by a cloud of dust and an army driver.

"Hop in! The Squadron's about two miles down the road," he said.

We climbed aboard and down the road we went. The German demolition squads must have worked overtime. The road was really torn up. However, it seemed no time at all until we arrived at the squadron area, which consisted of one big tent and about thirty small ones.

"Hey, George, what the heck are you doing here?" It was Ed Dombrowski - a navigator/bombardier I had met in Columbia, SC.

"Ed!"

"I ain't his brother."

"How long have you been here?"

"Got in about a week ago."

"See you in a minute or two," I replied, and after picking up our records, I reported to the Adjutant. He assigned us to our respective tents.

When Ed left Columbia, South Carolina, I never thought I would see him again. He was a big fellow and a boisterous one too, but one of the best navigators there. We were never intimate friends but our relationship was typical of fellows in the army. We would get drunk together every now and then, but that seemed about the only time our paths would cross. He was a big time operator and could usually top any experience you might relate. Occasionally he would get his stories mixed up, and when he realized that he was contradicting himself, he would laugh and say, "Oh hell, a man can't tell the truth all the time," and then he would start right in with another story.

I left for overseas about the same time Ed did, but got there a week later due to our layover in Algiers.

Gathering up my equipment, I started up the hill. Ed decided to come along and give me a hand. I was glad he did, for he was an old timer now and I was just as curious as a kitten.

"How many missions have you flown?" I asked Ed.

"Three."

"How are they, rough?"

"Not bad. Got shot up a little yesterday, but we were out of the flak in two or three minutes."

"Do they lose many planes?"

"No, the squadron hasn't lost one in the air in four months. They get shot up occasionally and now and then someone gets wounded or killed, but they don't lose any planes."

"Sounds good to me," I replied.

"I guess we're pretty lucky to be in this theatre," he said.

The tents had all been moved into a wooded area after a German raid of the base on May 13th -- except for one tent which remained in the open on the hillside. I was assigned to that tent. Those in the tent figured that if there were another attack, the Germans would never bother with a single isolated tent and they had spent too much time customizing it and getting settled in to move it -- a bit of insouciance that impressed me.

Such innocent insouciance would, of course, later be mocked by Joseph Heller (a member of the 488th Squadron which was also part of the 340th Bomb Group based at Alesan) in his novel, Catch-22.

Any reference to that tent, which my father believed to be quite similar to Yossarian's tent in Catch-22, always triggered a discourse by my father on Catch-22 and Joseph Heller – even if it did interrupt a telling of his own story.

Chapter Six
Catch - 23

Catch-23? Yep! Catch-23! It's quite simple: regardless of what you do or say or how you mock or pervert people or the facts, sooner or later, the truth will out.

If you believe that there really was a Catch-22 or Milo Minderbinder's syndicate, or guys who ditched planes on purpose, or C/O's who were irrationally obsessed with tight formations and bomb patterns, or that the Air Corps raised the number of missions one had to fly before completing a tour of duty just to mess with soldiers' minds, or that it's fine to whine incessantly about going into combat, or that it's humorous to mock those who served with you and who risked their lives for you every day, then you'd better believe that there is most definitely a Catch-23: do any of that and you deserve whatever comes your way and to be forced to fly every goddamned mission and then some - because it just wasn't so - and the truth will out!

Sure, there were absurdities in World War II and on Corsica in 1944. There are absurdities in every facet of life and the military is no exception - especially when you throw millions of men together from all parts of the country and all walks of life.

Heller would have everyone believe that the devastating German raid on the base at Alesan on May 13th - the remnants of which we had seen on the way in and the one and only raid against the 340th on Corsica - was precipitated by a fictional bombardier/profiteer, Milo Minderbinder, who was supposedly running a syndicate that made deals with the Germans in the middle of the war. What unadulterated crap! In point of fact, Axis Sally, the ex-American who spread propaganda on German radio, had announced in early May that a raid would be made on the 340th Group on Corsica in retaliation for the 340th's use of phosphorous bombs in advance of regular bombing runs - a practice the Germans claimed violated the Geneva Convention.

The phosphorous bombs were dropped by two or three advance planes that flew in at low altitudes and targeted enemy anti-aircraft gun positions. When the phosphorous bombs exploded, they caused the gunners' skin to itch and burn and, in theory, would prevent them from tending to their anti-aircraft guns during the regular bombing run. Even if the phosphorous bombs didn't hit the gun positions, just the fact that the advance planes came in targeting the German gun positions kept the gunners under cover for a few extra minutes which made the flak lighter and the missions safer. That's what prompted the German raid on Alesan – and that was straight from Axis Sally's mouth -- not some renegade syndicate run by an over-enterprising, traitorous American bombardier.

Were there enterprising bombardiers who did a lot of wheeling and dealing for supplies and who profiteered during their service? Sure. And there were pilots who did so, co-pilots who did so, radio gunners who did so, tail gunners who did so, ground crews who did so, and so on and so on. Yeah, those guys were there. But they were very few and far between and, like it or not, they also performed some rather decent services. If the Squadron was short on some supplies, they found ways to get them. They were scroungers – guys who could get you a spare starter or an extra ration or two of food or medicine if that's what was needed. Sometimes putting in a requisition just didn't work quickly enough. But what they didn't do and what nobody did or could do who served in a combat theater was to sell out their buddies and units to the enemy in the process. That may make a satire funny and salable, but it just wasn't so.

Guys also didn't ditch planes on purpose. Those planes kept us alive - especially the B-25's which we flew. They weren't the fastest or most agile of the medium bombers, but they were was the most versatile and the most rugged. They had twin engines and, more importantly, twin tails and rudders. You could lose one engine or one rudder and still get back to base. Yeah, those planes were, in my estimation, the best plane to take into combat because they got back – and they got back even when they were all shot up. There's not a pilot in his right mind who would waste one of those gems – not just to avoid a few days of combat. Any assertion of that is pure fancy. Nothing more!

Tight bomb formations and bomb patterns? Yeah, those became a religion in the 340th Group. Were they something to be mocked? Absolutely not! What everyone understood was that hitting targets was what would end the war as soon as possible. The principle is simple – the tighter the formation, the tighter the bomb pattern and the more targets that get destroyed and the shorter the war would be. And then we could all go home. But it wasn't just the C/O's who were obsessed with tight formations and bomb patterns. What I saw everywhere I went in the service from '43 to '45 and certainly in the 340th, was Americans being Americans – and that means always trying to make things better. We had bombardiers making adaptations to their bomb sights to improve accuracy. We had guys providing constant feedback on what design features of the planes worked, what didn't, and what needed to be modified – and those suggestions did make it back to the plants that produced the planes. The B-25's we flew went through seven basic models during the war and a whole bunch of sub-models – all of those derived from combat learning and modifications. The 340th pioneered the change from the manual release of bombs to radio-release. What that meant was changing from bombardiers visually watching the lead ship and then releasing their bombs immediately after those of the lead ship to a coordinated dropping of all bombs at one precise time by radio cueing. That, too, increased bombing accuracy and tight bomb patterns – but it also increased our success rate. Americans are an inventive and pragmatic people. They build better mousetraps. They build better tents, better latrines, better mess halls and better Officers Clubs and they build better bombsights. That's just what they do when left alone. And that's what happened during the war. Did improved bombing accuracy shorten the war? I'm sure it did...and if it was by just one day, it was worth it. Lives were saved and the terror shortened.

Yeah, as Heller claimed, the Air Corps did raise the number of missions required to complete a tour of duty several times. Big deal! We were fighting a war, not running a travel agency! They did what they had to do. We were fighting a war on a number of fronts and while replacement planes could be rolled off assembly lines at a pretty good clip, the same was not true of combat crews. Pilots and co-pilots required better than a year's training; navigator/bombardiers, six to nine months. And it takes 18 years from the birth of a pilot to his induction into the service. There simply weren't enough crews coming on line fast enough to send those already in combat home.

What would Heller have had the Air Corps do, send all of those with 30 missions home and let the Germans have the upper hand for the time it would take to get the replacement crews completely trained? Or would he have sent the replacements into combat before they knew how to fly the planes? The fact of the matter is that if we slacked off one bit and let Germany keep the war going until 1946, they would have had the atomic bomb and planes to deliver it to the Continental U.S.; they would have had jet fighters far better than anything we had in the works along with air-to-air missiles that could have taken out anything we could have thrown at them - including the B-29's we used against Japan. Again, the ratcheting up of minimum mission requirements made for funny satire, but mocking it was otherwise completely nonsensical. We were at war - and against the best war machine this planet had ever seen.

And whiners like Yossarian? You can whine in a free society and in a free country's army. You couldn't whine in the Luftwaffe or the German army. They shot their whiners and we all know what they did to others they didn't like. If a C/O of the 340th singled out a whiner for a few extra missions, I wouldn't be at all surprised and, in fact, I would think it entirely appropriate. I'd have sent them to the brig for a day or two.

Look, no one, or perhaps just a very, very few actually liked going into combat. It's hell. It's terror. It's death and the chance of it every time you go up there. It's seeing your buddies get killed and having to go on. There aren't any times out in war. I was anxious to fly my first mission. That was the last mission I was anxious to fly. But the war had to be fought and to do so, guys like me and everyone else in the 340th had to climb into airplanes and go get shot at and drop our bombs on bunches of guys on the ground who also didn't like getting bombed. It just had to be because if we didn't, Hitler was going to end up running the entire planet, exterminating or subjugating all of the races other than the German one, and ruling everyone with an iron fist...and shooting all the whiners. If you understood that, you crawled into your plane and did what had to be done...and you did it the best you could and you hoped or prayed that you didn't get killed in the process. Some of us were lucky and lived to tell about it. Hundreds of thousands did not.

Yossarian made a big point of the realization that they were shooting at him. So what? Everyone realizes that on their first mission or their first day at the front lines if they have half a brain in their head. Like it or not, war is personal. Everyone in combat is trying to kill each and every individual on the other side. Yossarian was dropping bombs whose purpose was to kill very specific individuals on the ground. He was shooting at them! And, in addition to those at whom we were aiming, others were going to get killed as well. Like it or not, civilians were killed by our bombs. Women and children were killed. Sometimes bombs don't fall exactly where they're aimed. That's war. It's not nice. Those facts don't help one sleep at night, but there's no changing them. Once a war is started, it plays out roughly the same as all other wars - a lot people get killed, some because they are being shot at and some because they just got in the way.

What was it really like in the 340th Bomb Group on Corsica in 1944? Were there memorable characters there? Absolutely! Again, that just happens when you draw your personnel from every corner of the country. I spent virtually every free waking moment when I wasn't training or flying combat up in the mountains or down at the beach fishing. Yes, fishing! In the middle of a war. I made my own poles, used the hook and line from my emergency kit and I took to the hills. I combed the surrounding area for trout streams and used the recreational Red Cross life raft at the beach for some offshore jigging. So what? No one was the worse off for it and it kept me balanced.

Were there guys, like Nately in Catch - 22, who fell in love with local whores? Sure. First, the women who became whores during the war were poor and had no other means of survival. Often their husbands, fathers, and brothers had all been killed. They were alone had no other way to survive. They did what they did to survive - nothing more, nothing less. They weren't bad people. They were just desperate. And some guys found things to love about them. So what? Is that mockable? I don't think so. War is life at the edge - at its most intense and pushed to the extreme. Winning is for the Generals and the countries. Doing one's job and surviving is for everyone else. From my perspective, if there was a Nately who found some love with someone in the middle of that death and destruction and that love got him through it, more power to him – and to her!

What I perceive was really behind Catch - 22 was nothing more than the old management/labor rift and antagonism. The management had a war to win. It was either that or death and defeat on a very grand scale. We, the laborers, had to go do it. Yossarian was a malcontented laborer. He worked when he had to, but he spent more time and energy trying to find ways to get out of work than he did doing it. We had them in the steel mill where I worked before and after the war and apparently, we had at least one of them on Corsica. There's always a gap between management and labor and there was a bit of a gap between officers, more so the commanders, and enlisted men. But quite frankly, I think we bridged it pretty well most of the time.

Everyone knows the old axiom that for every man in combat, there are ten men necessary behind the lines to support him. And the service of those ten is no less valuable. Not one bit! In fact, without it, the combat at the front lines can't occur. That was most definitely the case with the Air Corps and in the 340th on Corsica in 1944. I wouldn't fly a plane that didn't have a great ground crew keeping it perfectly maintained. Look, we got shot up a lot. When the planes came back, they had to be checked with a fine tooth comb for damage -- damage to all of the operating and control systems. First and foremost were the engines, but there were also the hydraulic systems, the electrical systems, and the bodies of the planes themselves. Yes, there were sheet metal guys who patched the flak holes – and we came back with a lot of those. If the ground crew guys missed something, friends died. Our lives were in their hands as much, if not more, than they were in the hands of the flight crews. Those guys were grease monkey-enlisted-men types if you want to call them that....but they were great! They were our friends and they were wonderful! They cared – cared about the planes and they cared about us. And they kept us alive. They knew their business and took care of it flawlessly. Hell, they not only fixed engines, they replaced entire engines – overnight and along with getting all the other routine maintenance done.

The armourers armed the planes and kept the guns and bombsights in working order. Try defending yourself with a jammed machine gun some time! The munitions guys lugged bombs from the dumps to the planes – and they worked at night when everyone else was sleeping so that the planes were ready to go every morning. And then they worked most of the day as well to get the next group of planes ready for the afternoon or evening missions.

The motor pool guys got us from camp to the planes and into town when we had the chance. The cooks cooked our meals and without food, nothing happens. The company clerk typed up the mission lists so that we knew who was flying and who was not, as well as all the operations reports which had to be filed daily. And the Commanding Officers had to schedule everything and everyone every day - and there were about 400 of us at any point in time. That's a lot of scheduling! And there were the docs who patched the wounded up and who also treated everything from flus and viruses to venereal diseases.

To be sure, the flight crews, especially the pilots, co-pilots and bombardiers, got most of the glory. We also got shot at on a regular basis where the others didn't. But without the others, we got nothing and we just might end up dead.

Those are the things that everyone understood. Every person supported every other and everyone knew it and everyone relied on it. That's how it really was. Not like Catch - 22, with C/O's refusing to see anyone, or with bombardiers running syndicates with the Germans, or with guys ditching planes, or Yossarians running around trying to whine their way out of combat - except for maybe one guy – Yossarian, whoever he really was.

It was also this way. Some guys never made it to combat. When my Squadron first headed overseas in 1943, they left with 14 planes. They lost three planes – and two crews, 12 men – along the way. One went down on the very first leg – from Miami to Puerto Rico. The other went down in the jungle. A third plane crashed on take-off in Brazil. No one was killed or injured in that one, but the terror that crew went through was no less than if they had crashed in combat.

The Squadron's first Commanding Officer was killed in combat within the first week. He didn't get killed by hiding in an office and not seeing anyone. He got killed because he was in a plane going into combat. He was already an ace before joining our Squadron as its first C/O. He was a very respected leader. And with him went the five others on the crew.

During the African campaign, my Squadron flew close ground support for Montgomery's British troops in the fight against Rommel. When you get hit flying low, the plane goes down and the crew gets killed. There's no room to recover. Had he been there at that time, I'm sure Heller would have whined about that or mocked the Desert Pink that the planes were painted - an effeminate color if ever there was one, but it worked. It was good desert camouflage.

But to mock the bureaucracy! That bureaucracy kept us alive. It kept us fed. It brought us mail! Mail! In the middle of a war! And God how we loved it! Movies and USO shows were great, but what really kept our morale up was the mail – the daily mail from home. When we lost planes, the bureaucracy got us new ones - often the same day! Our Squadron lost all its planes to the eruption of Mount Vesuvius in March of 1944 when the Squadron was based in Pompeii. In three days, the Squadron was back in the air with a whole new set of planes! The bureaucracy also kept us in fuel, bombs, other munitions, and men. The fuel alone for 15 planes flying one mission each a day each (and many days there were two or three) was about 5000 gallons. That's a lot of fuel and it has to get from the refineries and into combat day in and day out or we don't fly. Like it or not, it takes a bureaucracy to do that.

And the bureaucracy kept good records. Preventive maintenance was possible because the bureaucracy tracked every flying hour, every repair, and every part used on every plane and engine. And those records are even still available today! It takes a bureaucracy to coordinate the actions of several million men and thousands of airplanes and ships. Mock it? I embraced it then and still do today. I'm alive because of it.

But the ultimate insult of Catch-22 was mocking the men. I don't know who the models were for Heller's characters. I knew some good candidates. The Chief? Yeah, there was an Indian in our Group. I think he was an armourer - loaded bombs into airplanes. He was huge - about six feet five - and incredibly strong. He had the makings of a real Chief. Yet he was one of the gentlest and nicest people I've ever encountered. Was there anything to mock about him? Absolutely not! The man did his job very well and had more dignity than most men I've met in my life.

Major Major Major? That's an easy one, but I'm not going to get into names. Was he as Heller portrayed him? No way! Oh, he did push tight formations and bomb patterns – and in so doing, he made us one of the best goddamned Groups in combat anywhere.

Doc Daneeka? We had several flight surgeons who could have been the model for him. But again, if you needed to be patched up, they all did one helluva job.

Milo Minderbinder? We had several great scroungers, but not one traitor.

I wasn't in love with everyone I flew with or encountered on Corsica. But I would never mock them. Every damn one of them kept me alive. Men died over there. Mocking the living mocks the dead who served with them - and that's all Heller did.

No, what Heller did was not to wake anybody up to the absurdity of war or bureaucracy. He wrote a travesty of an account of what we did. He broke faith with those who put their lives on the line for him every day. He gave those who weren't there and who didn't understand what Hitler and the Third Reich were all about a basis for being anti-war and making whining a socially acceptable mindset. That's all he really accomplished -- to make whining fashionable. That and he made a lot of money off those with whom he served in the process. There was no real traitorous syndicate like that allegedly run by Milo Minderbinder. There was Joseph Heller and he sold out his comrades for money in a far more insidious way than Minderbinder ever allegedly did.

Heller flew his 60 missions and went home. For that he gets the respect that every combat veteran gets - every bit of it. But beyond that, I have no respect for him whatsoever. Catch - 22? No, there was no Catch - 22, just someone who turned on his comrades – and who did so long after the war was over when there was no one around to beat the living shit out of him.

If you believe in Catch - 22, believe in Catch - 23: sooner or later, the truth will out.

But enough of that…and back to the story.

Chapter Seven
Ed And I – The Jinx

I made up my cot that first evening and spent some time getting to know my tent mates, Bill Hale, Verl Miller, and Noble Byars, and BS'ing with Ed. I spent the following day straightening out the crew's records and learning the details of the organization.

The set-up seemed pretty good. I found the maintenance of the planes was wonderful, and that is good news to any pilot. The food left much to be desired, but was much better than the Infantry had been getting.

About two o'clock, I decided to walk over to Ed's and find out what the morning mission was like.

"Hi, Ed."

"Hello, George."

"Didn't wake you up, did I?"

"No, I was just lying here wondering what to do. Sit down."

"How was the mission today?"

"Milk run. There must be something big going to happen down at the beach-head soon."

"What makes you say that?"

"George, we've blown up every bridge between and Rome and Florence. As soon as Jerry gets one repaired, we fly over and blow it up again. I bet they haven't been able to move any supplies into Rome for the last two weeks."

"I'll be rather glad to get started, only I hope the first few aren't too rough."

"You're on tomorrow's schedule," Ed informed me.

"No."

"Yes."

"Well, I'll be darned. Are you sure of that, Ed.?"

"Yes. I'm sure, they haven't posted it yet but I was in Operations and saw it."

"Who'm I flying with?"

"Farnham."

"Who's Farnham?"

"He lives in the next tent. Pretty nice guy, and a good pilot, too."

"I think I'll walk by and see how my name looks in print."

"It's no use. The schedule won't be posted until four o'clock."

"No sense in going down, then."

"No, stick around. Maybe we can find a couple more fellows and get up a little game of poker."

I went to bed about nine o'clock that night and soon fell asleep. The night passed quickly. Dawn found me wide awake and as I lay on my cot, I suddenly realized that today was the day. I looked at my watch. Five-fifteen. There was still an hour before I had to get up. "Might as well have a smoke," I thought.

"What's the matter, George, nervous?" asked Verl Miller, a tent mate.

"No. Just a little excited."

"It's not so bad. One mission and you're an old timer."

Breakfast consisted of powdered eggs and bread. I ate the bread, and damned the man who invented powdered eggs. Then things started to hum.

Before I knew it, we were racing down the runway. We swung over the Mediterranean and skidded our plane into formation. There was Ed flying left wing. He waved. I smiled and waved back. Heading due east we started to climb four, five, eight, ten thousand feet. We leveled off. The day was perfect, not a cloud in the sky. I looked at my watch; nine-twenty. In thirty more minutes we would be over the target. It was supposed to be a rough one, near Cassino. I had read about them blowing up the monastery. It didn't seem possible that I was going to blow up some more of it. I noticed Farnham switch to interphone.

"O.K., boys, put on your flak suits," Farnham ordered.

We quietly obeyed. The engines droned on.

A black puff appeared in front of us. Flak. I suddenly realized that somebody was trying to kill *me*. I didn't like it. More puffs appeared. We seemed to be engulfed in a cloud of man-made fury - and there was nothing we could do. Once you pass the Initial Point of a bomb run, you're pretty much a sitting duck.

I felt the bomb bay doors open. The flak continued to burst around us. Our engines droned on. The lead ship released its bombs. Ours went immediately thereafter. I fervently hoped they killed every German down there. I now hated the master race. But the bombs were away and we could start evasive action. We started a sharp dive to the left 300, 350, 400 miles an hour; then we pulled straight up until every plane in the formation seemed to be standing on its tail. Again we dove, trying to squirm our way out of the flak. Things quieted down and we then turned our heading to due west, and started home.

I called the crew. "Anybody hurt back there?"

"No. We're all right; how about up front?"

"All O.K." I replied. The engines droned on.

"Well, Ed, what did you think of today's show?" I asked once we were back safe on the ground at Alesan.

"Pretty rough, but we all got back and I guess that's the important part."

"You're not on tomorrow's schedule, are you?"

"I haven't seen it. Are you, George?"

"Yeah, I'm on it but you aren't."

"Oh well, it doesn't pay to fly too much."

The mission the following day was perfect. No flak, no fighters. We flew over, dropped our bombs, circled around until the dust settled and viewed our handiwork. One more bridge blown to hell. I didn't mind fighting a war like this.

Ed was lying on his cot as I approached his tent.

"How was it, George?"

"Milk run, didn't even see one burst of flak."

"Maybe we aren't supposed to fly the same missions."

"Could be! Could be."

Ed flew the next day and I hung around the squadron area. Although I had been in combat only a few days and had flown only two missions, I felt like an old timer. In combat one learns quickly or one doesn't learn at all.

After dinner I walked over to Dick's tent, hoping to find that he was a fisherman.

"Hi, Dick."

"Hi, George."

"Say, Dick, do you ever do any fishing?"

"Down in Kentucky that's all we do all summer. Why?"

"Let's get a couple of lines from the Red Cross and go down to the beach."

"Let's go."

That afternoon I had my usual luck and sundown found us walking up the road towards the squadron area.

"Wonder what was the matter? I didn't have a bite all afternoon."

"I don't know, unless these foreign fish don't speak our language."

"I guess that's it, but I enjoy being out along the water."

"So do I, Dick."

Chapter Eight
Noble Byars

One of my tent mates was another co-pilot, Noble Byars. Noble was a southern fellow from Texas with a great sense of humor. He was also very short. Ha! Noble was so short –- not even five foot two -- that he had to use wood blocks on the peddles in the B-25's, but he could really handle an airplane!

On B-25's, there's a pilot and a co-pilot. The first pilot flies in the left seat and the co-pilot in the right. Generally, the pilot does the flying and the co-pilot does the checking – that and raising and lowering the landing gear for take-offs and landings. Every co-pilot's mission is to become a first pilot a.s.a.p. – and both Noble and I were on that same mission. While I liked Holley, the first pilot on my original crew, I felt that he did too much of the combat flying and I didn't feel I was getting the experience I needed to make it to first pilot. Within a week, I asked to be re-assigned to another crew or to float. That fit with the Squadron's desires – they wanted all pilots and co-pilots to be completely checked out in both roles. So I floated in combat and trained on my off days. I still liked Holley and my original crew; in fact, I talked to Holley and Semenak after each mission I flew. I just needed to get more experience to become a first pilot.

In my 30 days in combat, I flew 14 missions in 9 different planes with 5 different crews -- I flew most often with Wilbur Lantz, a Midwestern farmer from Indiana. Wilbur was a great guy and let me do much more of the combat flying. I was coming along very nicely.

Noble had been there a month when I got there. We started training together every chance we could get. Noble was checked-out as first pilot before I was, but he kept training with me to get me checked out as first pilot too.

Noble was also an avid fisherman. He and I started spending most of our free time rigging fishing poles and exploring the area around the base for fishing holes. Some days, we'd head up into the mountains and fish a trout stream or two. On others, we'd head down to the Mediterranean, commandeer the Red Cross raft or a small boat and fish the sea. Of course, we were fishing with home-made equipment and never did catch a damn thing except a few eels, but the important thing was to get away. Everyone deals with combat differently. In the air, you only see action every couple of days – but it's quite intense. You can spend your down time thinking about it way too much. I needed a diversion and fishing with Noble was mine.

At night, Noble and I would talk and tell stories. On one night, and there was only one such night the whole time I was there – the night I was finally cleared as a first pilot - we mixed drinks in our infantry helmets, got rather drunk, and spent the time telling jokes, stories, and singing hymns. We weren't scheduled to fly the next day. We sang all the hymns we could remember and stayed up until the wee hours of the morning. Neither of us were particularly religious or had particularly good voices, but we did sing enthusiastically -- as all Methodists, Southern or Northern, do.

At 6 am, I was awakened and told that I was flying. Someone had come down with something and had checked into the infirmary. I staggered from my cot, got dressed and reported for briefing. I was in no condition to fly, but grabbed some coffee at the mess, crawled into the plane, and tried to get my wits about me as best I could.

We took off and the pilot, I don't even remember who it was, immediately turned the controls over to me. He was sick as a dog with some virus but hadn't gone to sick bay. I had no choice but to fly the plane.

Somehow, I got into formation and was flying along just fine. Well, it was just fine until someone noticed that there weren't any other planes around – I had lost the formation! We were heading due east over Italy but had no idea where we were. We were sure that we were well behind the German lines. Alesan just lined up that way.

We had to drop our bombs somewhere since we could not return to the base from a mission with a live bomb load. We located a bridge and dropped our bombs. I believe that we hit it -- at least the bombardier said that we did. We turned around and headed on a reverse course home. As we were approaching Alesan, we spotted the Squadron planes and slipped in behind them and landed.

No one caught hell, but I did have to take a few extra training flights -- with Noble Byars, of all people, the guy I had gotten drunk with the night before. I never was sure what he was supposed to teach me. Regardless, it had been with Noble's help that I was cleared as a first pilot on June 14th. I was set, or so I thought.

Chapter Nine
Mail Call - Letters Home From The Front

Mail Call was the true highlight of every day in combat. The same was true on the home front. Letters were more precious than gold. They were the only connections with loved ones far away.

None of the letters my father received from home while overseas survived, but those that he wrote to my mother did. They wrote each other every day - sometimes more than once.

While the following 29 letters were focused on my mother, they also provide a good chronicle of his life at the base (writing about combat details was forbidden).

I've inserted some notes in italics or brackets which integrate his combat activities with the letters. References to missions, targets, and crews are from Squadron records.

Arrived on Corsica:

>Monday, May 22, 1944
>
>...here I am in Corsica and am fairly well settled. Everything is fine and I am still in good health. I am now sitting on my cot in my tent and the set up isn't bad at all. I didn't receive any mail today, but sure hope I get a batch of letters tomorrow. We didn't have a very long hop today so I am not too tired.

Tuesday, May 23, 1944

...here I am back again. It is now a quarter to four and I have just finished the most refreshing bath of my life (excluding dual). My bath tub was my G.I. Infantry helmet and you take it in stages and the grand finale is the cold water shave. By this time, my face has become accustomed to it and it doesn't bother me at all. At the present time, I am sitting on my cot which quite an affair of which I am very proud. On bottom is a half a pup tent, then three G.I. blankets doubled. Next is a mattress cover which I sleep in then three more blankets doubled on top of that and topped off by another half of a pup tent. My pillow is my jungle kit and it fills the bill rather well, a little hard, but much better than none at all. Sounds pretty cozy, don't you think?

I am in a tent with three other officers* and they all seem very nice. The name of the tent is 'Flack Happy' and the sign underneath it says "fathers and expectant fathers welcome." When they asked me my status, I told them I didn't know and would have to let them know later.

I have not received but one letter and sure hope the rest catch up with me pretty soon as the one is just about worn out from my reading it.

The food here is pretty good and when you consider everything in general, I would say very good.

*Note: Tent mates: Noble Byars, Verl Miller, and Bill Hale.

Wednesday, May 24, 1944

...here I am back again and today I am tired as a dog. I have had quite a full day. This morning, I got up around eight o'clock and right after breakfast, I got a shovel from supply and started digging in my fox hole and it is coming along fine. By eleven o'clock, I had five or six blisters on my hand and decided I had dug enough for today. Right after dinner, the tail gunner, Sgt. Donald Dick and the Radio man, Sgt. Carl Coombs, and I decided to go fishing and that we did. I rigged up quite an elaborate fly rod which I shall attempt to describe. On the end, I had a double snap – something like this [drawing] - and ran the line through it and back to the handle where I tied what I wasn't using and I had a spinner from our old emergency kit and I was really set. However, either they're weren't any fish or they weren't hungry because none of us even got a bite. I heard of another stream today that has quite a few mountain trout in it and will try that before too long.

My barracks bag that was shipped over by boat has not arrived yet, so you can expect all sort of stationary, but fear not, dearest, there'll be a letter every day come Hell or high water.

...it is now 9:30 and I just got back from a soft ball game. The pilots played the cooks and I played left field and made one hit and am really tired now. I think I'd better close now and hit the sack.

Thursday, May 25, 1944

It is now 2:15 and I thought I'd dash off a few lines to let [you] know just how everything was coming along. I just finished washing out a few things in my helmet and they are now out on the line. I dug a fireplace this morning, but ran out of ambition before I got it finished so expect to continue on with it in the morning, just what we'll use it for I do not know, but maybe some day I'll catch a couple of fish and we can have a fish fry. Sounds sort of nice doesn't it? I think I'll stroll over and see the gunner in a few minutes and see if I can talk him into going fishing this evening.

Last night, I played soft ball for the first time in quite a while and also managed to get a letter off to Fred and Helen. I will try to write to the rest of the folks in a few days. I haven't received my bag with all of the addresses in it so will you send me Beck's, Ray E.'s and Russ Cooley's? I think that he is over here some place and if possible I would like to look him up. Couldn't we really have a get together!

Notes: Fred and Helen are Harry's brother and sister-in-law.
Beck - Harry's sister, Army nurse, stationed in Burma.
Ray E. - Ray Eshleman, my mother's brother.
Russ Cooley - a friend from upstate New York.

Friday, May 26, 1944

Notes: 1st Mission - the Gustav Line near Monte Cassino, southeast of Rome;

Plane 7Z; Pilot: Stu Farnham; upon arriving in combat, crews were broken up for the first mission or two so that each new member could be checked out by an established member of the Squadron; Ed Dombrowski was also on the mission in a different plane.

...today, has been quite a full day for your husband. Arising at 6:30, the gunner, Sgt. Dick, and I took our fishing poles and a can of worms, got a command car and headed for the mountains. We went about fifteen or twenty miles and came upon the prettiest mountain stream you ever saw.

The water was as clear as glass and some of the pools were fifteen or twenty feet deep; after fishing for two hours and catching an 8 inch eel, we decided to quit. As soon as we put our tackle put away, a trout started to jump all over the place. That gave us the incentive to return which we shall do.

I was quite busy* this afternoon and after receiving my shot of whiskey, we returned and had supper. This evening, Holley, Joe, and I are going to take in the picture show. I believe the name of it is "Three Hearts For Julia" or something like that.

*Note: "busy" refers to a mission; shots of whiskey were issued afterward.

Saturday, May 27, 1944

Notes: Alternate Plane - no mission; Plane - 7X; Holley Pilot - Regular Crew. Alternate planes typically took off with the rest of the planes on the mission; if there were no problems with the other planes, the alternate plane returned to base.

...here it is Saturday evening and I am sitting on my sack and hoping to get this letter written before it gets dark. We drew our Px rations this evening and I got a couple of candy bars, a coke, a carton of smokes, a can of pipe tobacco, and a cigar. I sort of feel like a king in my own little way.

The food is still pretty good and I seem to be thriving on it. Tonight for supper, we had salmon, peas, canned peaches, pie and coffee. Doesn't sound half bad at all does it? I expect to eat part of one of my candy bars before I retire for the evening and that is something I sure miss - a snack before bedtime.

Our crew is back flying together again and making out all right.

Holley and I went to the show last night and it was really good. I had sort of a lazy day today and didn't get a whole lot accomplished except a bath taken and a shave.

Saturday, May 28, 1944

Notes: 2nd Mission: Railroad Bridge at Bucine - about 25 miles southeast of Florence; Plane 7V; Pilot - Holley; Regular Crew.

...here it is Sunday evening and it is really quiet and restful. We have the side of the tent up and there is a nice breeze blowing through. It is really lovely here in the evening and always reminds me of West Virginia.

I had a hair cut this evening and feel quite civilized again. I took a bath in my helmet around noon and also shaved and am very presentable at the present time. It is too bad you're not with me now as this is one of those evenings I would just like to sit with my arm around you and talk everything over, make a little love, and just sit there and congratulate myself on having picked a girl as lovely as you.

A bunch of mail came in today, but there was none for me, so I am patiently waiting and hoping every day to hear from you. They say once mail starts coming through, it is pretty regular so I hope by this time you have my permanent APO number. I am still reading the one letter I got from you when I was in North Africa and it is getting pretty well worn, but still as refreshing as ever.

May 29, 1944

Notes: 3rd Mission - Viaduct at Bucine - about 25 miles southeast of Florence; Plane 7D; Pilot - Holley; Regular Crew.

Here I am back again and it is now Monday evening and it is very lovely out today. Everything is so nice and quiet and it sort of puts a fellow in a peaceful mood. A little later, I intend to go down and take in a show. Deanna Durbin in *Honeymoon Lodge* is on and should be very good. We were going to go fishing this evening but have postponed it until tomorrow on account of the movie. It is nice to be able to get in a little fishing, sort of relaxes me and I just daydream.

Tuesday, May 30, 1944

Notes: 4th Mission; Railroad bridge - precise location unknown; Plane 7T; Pilot - W. B. Suthers.

...here it is Tuesday evening and is about eight fifteen and I'm starting my daily letter to my little wife. No mail came in today so I am mail-less still. I sure will be glad when it starts coming through.

I didn't get fishing today so I can't make a report today on how it was. If I'm not busy tomorrow, I may give it a try.

I am fine and still feeling good and enjoying my stay as well as can be expected.

This letter is now being written by candle light and if my memory serves me right, this is my first one. However, I honestly think I prefer good old electricity any day.

Wednesday, May 31, 1944

Notes: Practice; Plane 7L; Pilot W. B. Suthers.

...the month of May is about over and that means one month less that I will have to be away from you. Time seems to be passing fairly rapidly and I hope before we both can realize it, we will be back together again. Until that time, I want to receive a whole lot of nice long love letters from my little wife. I know you're awfully sweet , dearest, but I like your letters because they seem to draw me closer to you.

...since I've been in a couple of other countries, the picture has cleared itself up. They don't live, dear, they just exist and the dirt and filth that they put up with are almost [un]imaginable... I know we Americans are pretty big suckers, but we've also got a sense of right and wrong and as long as we're not afraid to fight for what we believe to be right, we'll be allowed to enjoy the benefits and privileges that we have.

Thursday, June 1, 1944

Notes: 5th Mission; - Road Bridge at Orte - about 36 miles north of Rome; Plane 7T; Pilot - W. B. Suthers.

PM Practice: Plane 7N; Pilot - Holley.

It is now seven thirty in the evening and I am quite tired today, however, this evening I received four letters and you can imagine how good that made me feel. Three were from you, honey, and one was from Beck. Your letters were dated May 5, 6, and 8 so I still got plenty coming to me. I was very glad to hear of your position at the hospital and know you'll get along all right. I was glad to hear that Don was so good and I wish the kid all the luck in the world and feel sure he will make out all right.

It was too bad about that plane crashing near West Chester and I am sorry it worried you, but, honey, I've told you to not worry like that about me.

Friday, June 2, 1944

Notes: Off Day.

It is now Friday and I was quite surprised to find that out. In my letter yesterday, I thought it was Tuesday, so you can readily see that days sort of get lost. I manage to keep the date straight in my mind, but never seem to know what day it is.

I spent the afternoon in the sack and at the present time am all slept out so I think I'll either go down to the show or down to the creek and do a little fishing. I don't believe I have ever told you about our theater, but it is quite an affair. It is built on a hill and everybody sits on the hillside and watches the show. There is a new regulation out that requires everyone to wear leggings and a head net at these performances so I will have to dig mine out if I go this evening. I don't know how you'll see through a head net, but I guess that is our problem.

You should see my lighting fixture. I got a piece of bamboo and rammed a candle into one end of it and stuck it into the ground near the head of my sack and it is very practical.

Saturday, June 3, 1944

Notes: 6th Mission - Perugia - between Rome and Florence in central Italy; near Lake Trusimeno; Plane 7T; Pilot - Holley; Dombrowski on the mission in a different plane.

PM Practice: Plane 7A; Pilot - Holley.

It is now nine p.m. and I am laying on my sack and writing this letter by candlelight and it is quite nice. Not as practical as electricity, but it sure fills the bill. I got up enough ambition a few minutes ago to shave and now feel quite like a gentleman. I am a little tired tonight but not too tired to write.

Tonight we drew our rations at our Px and I have four candy bars, cigarettes and accessories. I never seemed to crave candy as a civilian, but now that it is rationed, I really enjoy my bars. I haven't been doing any drinking except the double shot we get after a mission so I guess I'll have a good one coming to me, but I think I'll wait until I get the urge.

I have been doing a little reading since I have been here and I read one book that was really good. The name of it was "Mr. Winkle Goes To War" and it was really funny. I believe I told you that I finished "The Robe" and it is making the rounds. It was undoubtedly one of, if not the best book I have ever read.

Sunday, June 4, 1944

Notes: 7th Mission - target location unknown; Plane 7L; Pilot - S. Lovinfosse.

PM Practice: Plane 7S; Pilot - Lovinfosse; Bombardier - Dombrowski.

It is now Sunday evening and as I lay on my sack and open this letter to my wife, I can look back on a very full day.

I had some sack time this afternoon and for supper we had chicken and, honey, it sure was good. Right after supper, Noble Byars, who is a Lt. tent mate of mine, and I went down to the little creek that empties into the sea near us and did a little fishing. I caught a little eel about six or eight inches long and that was all. We want to get up to the mountains again before long as that was a beautiful stream and I know there are trout in it.

In the afternoon, we went down the road a couple of miles to an outdoor shower where they have hot water. Man, did it feel good to stand under a shower again really lather up. I washed my head and believe you me it really needed it and I intend to go down there regularly from now on.

Monday, June 5, 1944

Notes: No letter. AM - 8th Mission - Road Bridge at Narni - about 40 miles north of Rome; Plane 7L; Pilot - W. C. Lantz.

PM Practice (afternoon); Plane 7S; Pilot - Lovinfosse; Bombardier - Dombrowski.

9th Mission (evening) - Road Bridge at Orte - about 36 miles north of Rome; Plane 7X; Pilot - W. C. Lantz; HDG later awarded Air Medal for this mission; Dombrowski on same mission in different plane.

Tuesday, June 6, 1944

Notes: Off Day. No letter.

Wednesday, June 7, 1944

Notes: AM Practice: Transition; Plane 7X; Pilot - W. C. Lantz.. PM Practice: Radio Bombing; Plane 7S; Pilot - W. C. Lantz..

...I must apologize for not writing you yesterday.* It was the first time I had missed but I had quite a full day. [Yesterday,] I fooled around in the morning without much to do and at noon, we were told that we had the rest of the day off so Noble Byars, Sgt. Dick, another Sgt. and I took off fishing. We went down the road about ten miles and found a beautiful stream. One of the enlisted men gave me a box of flies and several hooks so I felt very confident of getting my limit.

It was a fair size mountain stream and we saw a bunch of brook trout about a foot long, but we tried everything to get them to but it did no good at all. We could see them, but darned if we could catch them. We fished about five miles of the stream and while I enjoyed it immensely, I would have like to have tied into a couple.

On our way home, we stopped at a French wine bar and had a couple of glasses of vino and then got a hop on a truck back to camp. There was a case of C rations on the back and as it was past supper time, we each took ourselves a can and upon our arrival at camp, we gathered around the little fire place that I had built and we cooked supper like we were Camp Fire Girls… and it was really good.

*Notes: Actually, missed writing for two days: June 5 and 6. June 5th was very busy - two missions plus practice in between.

Here I am back again for the second time today. It is now ten thirty p.m. but as the other fellows are still writing, I thought I'd dash off a few lines to you to sort of make up for missing yesterday. This is being written by candle light.

This morning, I got a very lucky break. At the present time, I am flying with a boy named Lantz and he and I went up and got some transition (training) time. He let me do almost all of the flying and I even shot a few landings and made out all right. It sure made me feel good that they are giving me the opportunity to learn a little more about this ship.

I don't know whether I have told you or not, dearest, but this squadron is composed of the finest bunch of fellows I have ever met and I sure feel lucky to be one of them. They have a marvelous record and have received several citations for the work they have done. There is practically no chicken sh__ here and that suits me to a tee. The army is much different overseas and, in my opinion, much better.

Thursday, June 8, 1944

Notes: Off Day

I got paid today and as I still have most of the money I came over with, I am enclosing three money orders for one hundred dollars each, which, of course, totals $300. This should make a very nice start on our bank account and you needn't worry about me having enough money as I still have almost a hundred dollars left and all you can spend is about two dollars a week excluding poker games which as yet I have not tried over here. My allotment wasn't effective until June 1 and I just got paid for May so there was nothing deducted except my bond and insurance. Next month, they will only deduct $100 for my class "E" allotment, so I'll more than likely send a money order for the balance. Effective July 1, the class E allotment will be $175 and at that rate we should really have a nice little nest egg for after the war and may be able to buy a little home of our own or at least be able to make a decent down payment on a home. Just think of having a place of our own that we can fix up and be able to realize that it's all ours. Maybe Grandfather Copeland will want to sell his place in Westwood and as we both liked it so much, maybe we'll be able to get it.

I didn't fly today and after getting up at seven thirty for breakfast, I decided to catch up on my correspondence.

Right after supper, Noble Byars and I went down the road and took a hot shower and upon returning to our tent, I had a very good shave and even combed my hair. Now I feel right and ready but you are there and I am here, so I guess it'll have to wait.

Friday, June 9, 1944

Notes: 10th Mission - Road Bridge at Orvieto - about 56 miles north of Rome; Plane 7Z; Pilot - W. C. Lantz.

...here it is Friday evening again and Noble Byars and I have just returned from a very pleasant evening of fishing. We went down to a little creek and followed it down and it was lovely. We could see a whole bunch of fish and they were jumping all over the place. They have one of those life rafts down there and they sure are swell for fishing. I fly fished all over the place, but they just didn't seem to want flies. Then we tried earth worms, but they still didn't give us any consideration.

About that time, an enlisted man came down along the bank with a bass about seventeen inches long. He had shot it with a rifle and when we got to talking to him, he told us that he was really after minnows and that they went out onto the Mediterranean about a hundred feet and he had caught a sea bass that weighed ten pounds yesterday. So out to sea paddled your husband and his fishing buddy, Noble. The fish in the Mediterranean were not hungry this evening so again we returned empty handed but at peace with the world. There is something about going out fishing that relaxes a fellow and gives him time to think. The next time we go, we are going to make an effort to get some minnows and I hope to be able to report a little better luck.

Saturday, June 10, 1944

Notes: 11th Mission - Fano Railroad Marshalling Yard on the eastern coast of Italy - about 22 miles south of Rimini; Plane 7B; Pilot - W. C. Lantz.

Saturday evening and here I am over here and there you are back home. How I would like to be with you tonight and take in a show and then maybe go up to Frank Pelzers for a few drinks. Maybe I'd have a few too many and you'd drive home, but, oh boy, when we got there... A guy can dream can't he?

...Since they have started the second front, it may mean that it will be over before too long, but I imagine it will take a little while as Jerry is a tough fighter and he has had a long time to prepare for this.

This letter is being written by the light of five candles which are in a very unique holder which Bill Hale, one of the boys in the tent made. It is all out of bamboo and really throws a nice light. They seem to have a good supply of candles so we have no kick at all. Tonight, we drew our Px rations for the week and I got four candy bars, four cigars (two of them El Productos), a box of sugar candy, and two packs of chewing gum. Not half bad at all do you think?

I sent the mattress cover that I have been sleeping in to the laundry and am now snuggling in between G. I. blankets and don't mind it at all as they are nice and warm.

Sunday, June 11, 1944

Notes: Off Day.

Sunday evening and it is now nine thirty and I'm laying on my sack and starting my letter to my wife. I didn't fly today, but arose at seven-thirty, ate breakfast and at ten o'clock went to church. It was a very nice service and you sure appreciate just what it's all about. The chaplain is a wonderful speaker and has a way of putting his message across. We had corn beef, potatoes, peas, and carrots, and pineapple and it was very good. This afternoon, I had a session on the sack for a few hours and after both energy and ambition returned to me, I arose and took my pen knife and started to work on a tin tobacco can and fashioned myself two drones (spinners).

After supper, Byars, Dick, Sgt. Jones and myself took off down the road to try our luck with the fish. We weren't able to get the rubber boat, so we fished from a raft which was made up of four gasoline barrels welded up to a couple of pieces of steel. It was the same old story, however. We could see schools of fish and they were jumping all over the place. Some of them were around fifteen inches long and weigh a couple of pounds. They are some sort of sea bass and I sure hope to get a couple before too long.

At the present time, it is raining to beat the devil and this tent is strictly a fair weather tent and this paper is really getting spotted up. The candle has not gone out yet but is really flickering around in the breeze.

It is really raining to beat the devil and this paper is soaked but *c'est la guerre* as the French would day. I had to move my bed and may wear water wings to bed. I am glad we are on top of a hill and I bet the boys down at the bottom are getting washed away.

Monday, June 12, 1944

Notes: AM Practice: Transition; Plane 7J; Pilot - W. C. Lantz. PM Practice: Transition; Plane 7Z; Pilot - W. C. Lantz.

...today was quite a red letter day for your husband. I received three letters from you and a Lukens Plate*. All of the mail was forwarded from my temporary APO number but I was so glad to hear from you. I am awfully glad you liked your stockings and I am so glad they fit you. Today was the first I knew that you weren't pregnant and you can rest assured as soon as I get back to the States, we'll take care of that. Your letters were dated May 19, 21, and 22.

* *Note: the company magazine of Lukens Steel Co.*

None of your mail has been censored and I don't think they bother much with mail coming out of the States.

They are giving me a swell break by giving me transition training. Today, I flew left seat for the first time and shot three landings and made out fairly well. This afternoon, I landed from the right side. I sure am glad they are giving me this break.

Tuesday, June 13, 1944

Notes: No letter. 12th Mission Railroad Bridge at unspecified location; Plane 7P; Pilot - W. C. Lantz.

Wednesday, June 14, 1944

Notes: PM Practice: Plane 7P; Pilot - Noble Byars.

It is now --- that's all the further I got last night. It was midnight when I started. We had been to the movies. It was Bing Crosby in *Going My Way*. At least I think that was the name. He played the part of a priest and it was a marvelous show.

This morning we were up early, got a car, and headed for the mountains. Again, we didn't catch anything and about noon we went in swimming bare and it was wonderful. The mountain stream was as clear as a crystal and nice and cool.

When we got back to camp, Lt. Byars and I went up and flew some transition. He is also a co-pilot but I have been checked out as a first pilot and I am making out fairly well. I'm not a hot rock, but for all the time I've had in the ship, I think I do all right. We shot a few landings and both of us made out O.K. Understand now, dear, I'm not flying first pilot in combat, just on training missions, but that's a big help. They really treat us swell over here. We are going to try and fly all of our practice missions together as we both like each other's flying and he is the one who accompanies me on all of my fishing trips and is one swell fellow. He is from Texas and we really get along.

Note: The handwriting begins to seriously deteriorate.

I don't know whether you have guessed it or not....but we are killing a quart of rum tonight (three of us) and I'm starting to feel it. I guess I'd better close now and we will mix up another drink and drink to your health.

Thursday, June 15, 1944

Notes: Alternate Plane: flew 13th Mission: Viaduct at Castagna; Plane 7P; Pilot W. C. Lantz.

...here I am back again today with a beautiful hangover. Three of us consumed a quart of run last night and we really had a time. I wrote you a letter after we had started to drink and to be truthful about it, I can't remember what I wrote. After a few drinks, we started singing and it ran into the wee hours of the morning. I guess we kept half of the camp awake but it was well worth it as I hadn't hung one on since I left the States.

I received two letters today and a birthday card.

I am going to wash up when I finish this and shave. I have been shaving every day and my face is used to cold water by this time. Tomorrow, Noble Byars and I are going to make a minnow net, try and get a few minnows and see if we can get these darned fish to bite. We have tried everything else and nothing seems to work. I sure wish you were here, dearest, to accompany me on our little fishing trips. The water is beautiful and you can see all the fish you want to but I'll be darned if they'll bite.

Friday, June 16, 1944

Notes: Off Day

...here it is Friday again and Noble Byars [and I] spent the day in the mountains and had wonderful time. As usual, we didn't catch a darn thing. As a matter of fact, we didn't even see anything (fish) today. After spending a few hours fishing, we decided to go up to a town that we had never visited and it sure was wasted time. Any town outside of the States just isn't worth seeing. We came back and went down and laid on the beach. Mail came in today, but there was none for your husband. I sure will be glad when your mail starts coming through to me direct.

It is now seven p.m. and I am sitting on my sack and this evening it is pretty warm. I just finished a complete bath in my helmet and shaved and put on clean underwear and stockings and now feel very clean.

We are all sitting here batting the breeze around and every time I start a few lines, somebody starts recounting an experience and by the time they finish, I have forgotten what I started to write. It will be much easier to write to you when your mail is fairly recent. While I happen to think of it, I must tell you about the dogs we have here. I don't know how many there are but there are *G.I., Damn It, Rosie* (the little lady who welcomes all new comers), *Fluffy*, and *Red*. Little *Damn It* is just a pup and is the spitting image of Vic and has the same type of disposition. He and I have become quite friendly.

Saturday Evening, June 17, 1944

Notes: Off Day

Today, I received your first letter addressed directly to me here at the 487th. I sure was glad that it finally started to come through and I imagine and hope it starts coming through.

I am glad that there is practically no place over here to spend much money and I am able to send a good bit home. I want us to have a nice little nest egg so we will be able to settle down and have a nice little place of our own and not have to stretch every penny getting started again.

I want to really make things nice for you, dearest, and we'll have a nice big family and really settle down and enjoy life and each other. Since I have been separated from you, I have realized more than ever just what life is supposed to be all about.

Sunday Evening, June 18, 1944

...today the weather has been bad and I didn't fly and, in my opinion, I believe I have made the most of it. I was out of the sack long enough this morning and then crawled back into bed and caught up on my sack time. After dinner, we fooled around and then I got a letter off to your grandmother and one to Beck and then right after supper, Noble Byars, Horace Jones and I went down to the swimming hole and tried a few spinners, but again had no luck. We came back and decided to cook some food and we had a small class feast and I really feel fine. It isn't every night that I eat before I hit the sack, but I really do like to go to bed full, so I guess I can look forward to a good night's sleep.

At the present time, the fellows are sitting around and shooting the bull and I am writing this by candle light. I imagine I will have to get used to electricity again.

Well, dearest, it is about eleven o'clock now and I guess I'll undress and catch a few winks of sleep.

Monday Evening, June 19, 1944

Notes: Off Day

Although it is only five p.m., I thought I would start my letter and more than likely finish it up later in the evening. Mail came in today and although there was none from you, I did get V-mail letters from Frankie Marino and one from Helen thanking us for the clothes hamper. I was sure glad to hear from both of the them. Frankie gave me all of the gossip and also the status of the office. I was sure sorry to hear that Maurice Lambert's ship went down in the Mediterranean and hope he got out all right. The weather has been bad again today and I didn't get much done except to go up the road this morning and take a shower, eat, and hit the sack for the balance of the day. I guess I should write a few more letters, but I have answered all I have received so far and in that way, I think I'm keeping up. I do want to get a few lines off to Aunt Ella before too long and as you have sent me Kip's address, I believe I'll write him this evening or tomorrow.

We didn't go fishing today, but will more than likely be out after them before too long. We haven't tried minows (I guess there should be two "n's" in that) as yet, but imagine we'll really snare a big batch of them when we do. The big problem is where to get the minnows.

I just got back from the hospital. I went up to see Jim Cordell. He is the Engineer who came over with us. He got hit in the hip with a piece of flak the other day. It wasn't too serious and he should be back with us in a few days. I still have a bar of candy left and expect to devour it tonight. I never cared much for candy back in the States, but it is a treat over here.

Tuesday, June 20, 1944

Notes: Practice: Transition; Plane 7C; Pilot W. C. Lantz.

Another day, another two hours training and that is about all to report today. Haven't been fishing or swimming for the past couple of days and at the present time am well caught up on my sack time. After a few more days, I guess Byars and I will take off fishing again and spend the day in the mountains. I sure wish you could accompany me. Just imagine me being able to make love to you in the picturesque setting of a Corsican mountain. However, I would settle for any place just to be with you, dearest.

Sgt. Dick just stopped in and handed me an air mail letter from Fred. It was dated June 7 and I sure was glad to hear from him. He writes an awfully interesting letter and has been writing once a week regularly and I sure am glad of it. I guess I have been getting about a letter a week off to him.

If you can possibly get a hold of some film, will you send it to me even if it's just one roll. I kick myself in the pants every time I think about my sending the film you had gotten me over in my barracks bag because I have my doubts if I will ever get it. But such are the disadvantages of not knowing.

Wednesday, June 21, 1944

Notes: Alternate Plane: did not fly; Plane 7J; Pilot - Tom Casey. Last letter before being shot down June 22.

Darn small paper isn't it? But I was able to get a little of this today and it is writing paper, so I got what I could. We went up to a small town today and drew our Px rations there instead of in our squadron. They just started this and it is a much better set up. We have a larger selection of things and I bought all I could. Even got three pairs of stockings and two pairs of underwear and a pair of shoe strings plus four bars of candy, 24 cigars, two packs of smokes (I have practically a carton), so that's all I needed, foot powder and two cans of orange juice. Not bad for combat would you say?

This evening I also managed to take a bath and put on all clean clothes and really feel the gentleman flyer, sitting around writing my sweet little wife and smoking a big cigar.

I received three letters from the States today. Two from you and one from Frankie Marina. Your letters were dated June 7 and June 8 and that's not bad at all. It sort of tickled me when you said my days and the corresponding dates didn't tie up. I have a time with that. If I get the day right, then the date is usually wrong, but I try hard. I was glad you sent me Russ Cooley's address. I must write him and if he is any way near me, maybe I can get a few days off or vice versa and see him. I sure would like to be able to bat the breeze around for an evening or two.

You mentioned the fireplace I had built, well, dearest, it has been put to good use. Only I must confess we haven't had our fish fry yet, chiefly because we haven't caught any fish. However, canned "C" rations taste pretty darned good and some of the boys brought some canned goods with them from the states when they came over and we have been doing them justice.

You asked if there was anything you could send me such as cigarettes, etc. No, dearest, we get plenty cigarettes (a carton a week) and that is more than I smoke. I have mentioned before, dear, but I could use some film if you can get a hold of any.

Chapter Ten
Ed And I - The Proof

"What do you say, George?" Ed greeted me.

"Hello, Ed. How was it today?"

"Nothing to it; got a little flak but they must have been low on shells. I only counted four bursts."

"Seen tomorrow's schedule?"

"Yes, we're both on it; makes number nine for me."

"It will be number six for me."

"I didn't know you had that many, George."

"Creeping right up on you, old man."

The target was Perugia, a small Italian city, and it was a rough one. Our plane got shot up a little but we were not in any serious trouble. Two men in Ed's plane were seriously injured by flak and he was upset all evening.

"Well, Ed, it was a little rough today, wasn't it?"

"You aren't just kidding. One of the guys in my plane had his foot just about blown off and another just got hit all over. They'll both be OK, but..."

"That's too bad, but at least they got back."

"If you're going to get it, you're going to get it; so I guess there's no use worrying about it."

"You can say that again, brother."

We didn't fly on the same missions for the next week or so, then one evening, June 21st, Ed stopped by my tent.

"Did you see tomorrow's schedule yet, George?"

"Yep"

"Am I on it?"

"Yep."

"You?"

"Yes, brother, I'm on it. You're on it and to make things even better, we're both in the same plane!"

"I don't like that, George. It's rough enough when we're both on the same mission, but both in the same plane...that's too much!"

"You're not superstitious, are you?"

"Maybe I am and maybe I'm not, but I still don't like it."

"That's all imagination."

"Maybe so."

"I wonder where we'll go tomorrow."

"It doesn't matter as long as we don't go back to Cassino."

"That was a little too rough."

After I jumped and opened my chute on June 22nd, I knew Ed was right. It was just too much -- both of us in the same plane.

Chapter Eleven
June 22, 1944

There I was at 10,000 feet over Italy...

This was the opening line I had heard so many times in my life. I thought I was prepared for what was coming next - one of my father's standard behind-the-lines stories. It wasn't. This time, he recounted what happened on June 22, 1944 when he was shot down. I was soon on the edge of my seat.

We were bombing a railroad bridge at Gricigliana (Gri-chil-yana) on the main rail line running south from Bologna to Florence.

That bridge was a tough target -- a short, single-track bridge nestled in a very narrow valley between two steep mountains. It was a crucial target. That rail line was the main supply line for the German troops to the south. For much of its length, it was protected by tunnels. Flat stretches of track are more easily hit, but they are also more easily and quickly repaired. Taking out the bridge at Gricigliana would disrupt German re-supply efforts for some time. That, in turn, was crucial to winning the battle on the ground at the front just north of Rome. That was our job – blowing up road bridges, railroad bridges, and marshaling yards to keep the German re-supply efforts paralyzed.

That afternoon found us gathered around our plane, 7C, a B-25 named *McKinley Junior High*. It was named in honor of the junior high school in Muncie, Indiana that had raised the $250,000 needed to finance it by selling war bonds. It was a brand new B-25J which had just arrived in combat not more than a month before. It was still unpainted.

All seemed a little quieter than normal before a mission. We had just come from the briefing and the briefing officer had not painted a very rosy picture of what was in store for us. The target was protected by twelve batteries of

German eighty-eight millimeter guns. The 340th Bomb Group, my Group, had tried to destroy this bridge on three previous occasions the last of which had been just a few hours before. All three attempts met with disastrous results – a lot of planes shot up and damaged by flak - yet the bridge remained intact.

As a result of our misses, the Germans also knew our attack pattern and altitude -- from the west at 10,000 feet.

I was flying with another crew, replacing their regular co-pilot who was ill with some sort of crud. I was a floater – filling in wherever I was needed. Tom Casey was the pilot. I'd never flown with Casey before. We were together the day before on the alternate plane, but didn't fly the mission. I only knew Casey through Ed Dombrowski, the bombardier on Casey's crew and a drinking buddy of mine from our training days in South Carolina. Casey was good and thorough and had Ed's trust. That was enough for me.

"'Let's go, fellows, there's the signal from the tower,' I said.

We crawled into the plane and I started the engines. We taxied onto the runway and took our position in the line. We took off from Alesan, Corsica around 6:30 PM. After the formation had been assembled, we headed northeast.

The day was ideal. The Mediterranean was spread out before us like a carpet of blue velvet. It seemed hard to realize that we were on a mission of destruction and that before long, man would be pitted against man with two of his deadliest instruments of hate: thousand-pound bombs and anti-aircraft guns and their flak.

We were in the second of two boxes from the 487th Squadron. The 310th Group also had three boxes of six planes right ahead of us -- 30 planes total on the mission. We approached the target at about 7:15 PM.

"Put on your flak suits, boys," Tom Casey, the pilot, commanded over the interphone as we approached the target.

"I've had mine on since we took off," was the tail gunner's reply.

The flak was very heavy and accurate, exploding precisely at 10,000 feet.

From the IP, the Initial Point of a bomb run, the planes had to be flown precisely straight and level until the bombs were released. That was crucial to bombardiers' sighting and hitting the target. We also had to tighten up the formation - to be sure we hit the target. No evasive action whatsoever was allowed. Those two or three minutes were the terror-filled times on every mission and this was one of the worst. We were goddamned sitting ducks -- especially those of us at the back of the formation.

Dombrowski was the bombardier. That worried me. Oh, Ed was a fine navigator and bombardier and a good friend -- a fellow Pennsylvanian nonetheless -- we even had the same birth date of all things -- but every time we were on the same mission, it was a rough one...and here we were assigned to the same plane! We gave our wallets to the ground crew before leaving Alesan -- that's how sure Ed and I were that this one was going to be rough.

Ahlstrom was the radio/gunner. He was OK too. His station was right behind the cockpit. He did radio duties normally, but he'd also be the gunner in the top turret if we were jumped by German fighters. I didn't know the waist gunner, Kaplan, or the tail gunner, Obravatz. I had just arrived in combat one month before and still didn't know all of the four hundred or so men in the Squadron, the 487th.

The planes ahead of us were engulfed in black smoke. I could see the bombs leave the lead ship. Ours quickly followed. The instant after we dropped our bombs, we were hit by flak. Our plane shook as though it were trying to tear itself apart. The left engine had been shot away. Another screaming report filled the plane. We were hit amidships. I looked around. Fire was sweeping back through the plane. The fuel lines had been hit and it wouldn't be long until the tanks would blow. The hydraulic lines were also hit and the hydraulic assists for the flight controls were lost -- like losing power steering in a car. The right engine was sputtering and coughing. Shortly thereafter, it started running away -- a pilot's worst nightmare because at some point, the prop speed would become too great for the blades and they would disintegrate and fly off -- possibly into the plane and they were right next to the cockpit - not more than a foot away!

The pilot, Casey, who was sitting about six inches to my left, was hit in several places by the flak. Part of his head was missing. His blood was everywhere -- splattered all over the inside of the windshield.

I took the controls and issued the order to jump over the interphone. It was all I could do to keep the plane level. Without any hydraulic assist, it's just brute strength against all the forces acting on the control surfaces of the plane. Keeping the stick under control took every ounce of strength my arms had -- and the rudder pedals were no easier. I tried to kill the right engine, but it was too late -- those controls were gone as well. The best I could hope to do was to keep the plane level for as long a time as possible so that the rest of the crew could get out. That's what I did.

We were really on fire! Both the hydraulic and fuel lines crossed the plane amidships and both were spewing their highly flammable fluids into the plane. The fire was in front of the bomb bay -- right behind us. The flames went up and out through the top turret. It was intense and raging. Three of crew I had trained with, my buddies, Holley, Semenak, and Dick, were in the plane behind us and the flames were dancing on the nose of their plane several hundred feet back. We were in deep trouble.

Obravatz, the tail gunner, called over the interphone that Kaplan, the waist gunner in the tail section behind the bomb bay, was dead and that he was jumping. Obravatz went out the rear escape hatch.

Ahlstrom was in the middle of the fire. He had his harness on, but not his chute -- it was lying on the floor. I don't know how he did it, but he went down into that fire to retrieve his chute and to open the front escape hatch. That small 24-inch square door in the floor was our only way out. Ahlstrom's clothing was on fire. He couldn't get the hatch open.

Ed Dombrowski didn't hear that Kaplan was dead or the order to jump - he didn't have to. From his position in the glass nose of the plane, he could see the damage and knew we were going down. He crawled back from bombardier's position in the nose of the plane through the tiny crawlway under the cockpit and into a wall of fire. He threw Ahlstrom aside and went at the hatch. Ed was a big 200-plus pounder and strong as an ox. He struggled hard and finally forced the hatch open.

The fire was causing our own ammunition to detonate inside the plane. The flames had completely melted the top turret. That left the two 50-caliber machine guns, each with it's own ammunition belt, right in the middle of a natural chimney. The shells were firing in every direction. I was grazed on my nose and my left shoulder -- by our own ammunition!

By then, Ahlstrom was completely on fire and burning up. And he was right in the middle of the detonating ammunition. I don't know whether he was hit or not, but can't imagine that he wasn't. When Dombrowski got the hatch open, Ahlstrom jumped -- completely engulfed in flames. I understand that he did get his chute on, but it either failed to open or he wasn't alive to open it. All I know is that it never opened. Dombrowski was also on fire -- even his hair was burning like a torch. Ed had his chute on and he went next.

I was using every ounce of strength I had to keep the plane under control, to get it safely out of the formation, and to keep it level while we were descending. We were starting to lose speed and altitude fast. I looked over at Casey and figured him for dead. No one could be alive with that much of his head gone. Just then, he turned his eyes toward me and said, in one last act of heroism, "For God's sake, George, get out!" and died. I climbed out of the seat, stood there for a second or two at the most, and went down through the fire and out the hatch.

I remember Casey's and Ahlstrom's heroism. And Kaplan's. And Dombrowski's. Those were my heroes and all but Dombrowski and Obravatz died. And me...I was lucky.

My father paused for a moment and closed his eyes. To remember. To honor. There were tears. Tears for those who died, those he barely knew, but with whom he had risked his life while they lost theirs. They had taken forty-six years, those tears, but they were, I thought, quite therapeutic.

Finally, he broke the silence with a laugh.

Ha! I had refused parachute training. I was a young smart ass and thought that parachuting was too damned dangerous to practice. If my life depended on it...well, then I'd jump, but not just for the hell of it. How much could there be to pulling a rip cord?

Well, I jumped once and only once in my career -- on June 22, 1944.

I knew enough not to pull the cord immediately. Some guys panic and pull it too soon and end up getting the chute caught in the plane. I waited at least 10 seconds before I pulled the cord.

Nothing happened!

"Ah, shit!" I thought "I survived getting hit bad in the plane and was now going to die because my goddamned chute didn't open."

I felt something brushing against my face. I swatted at it. It didn't go away. I swatted at it again and then several seconds later realized that it was the small pilot chute which pulls the main chute out of the sack. It was stuck and without the pilot chute, the main chute won't deploy. I pulled on it and it sailed up and away pulling the main chute out right behind. What a relief!

Everything happened so fast. We had probably lost two thousand feet in altitude by the time I jumped. Between waiting to pull the rip cord and the problem with the pilot chute, I had probably lost another six thousand feet. I was about two thousand feet from the ground when my chute finally opened. There isn't a lot of sky or time left at two thousand feet.

I looked to the west and could see Ed's chute disappearing behind the mountain. He had opened his chute much higher and was drifting with the wind in the other direction. He was going to be on one side of the mountain and I was going to be on the other.

I looked at the plane. Not only had most of the left engine been blown away, with the hydraulics gone, the left landing gear had come down. Most of the left tail and rudder were gone as well. I'd heard about a B-25 getting back to base on one engine and one tail with no hydraulics, but it had taken both the pilot and co-pilot struggling with all of their might to do it. I felt good that alone I had been able to keep the ship out of a spin and flying level for long enough for everyone who was alive to get out.

The way we were hit – with the left side decimated - the plane wanted to spin out immediately. Once a plane goes into a spin, the crew gets pinned against the inside of the fuselage by the centrifugal force of the spin and the force of the acceleration downward – and there they stay until their death when the plane crashes. They don't get out. That's not a pleasant way to go. I had done well. I had done my job when I had to do it – when lives were on the line. That's what it was all about.

The plane's right engine or wing tank exploded shortly after I jumped and the plane was screaming toward the ground to the south of me. I couldn't watch the crash and turned away.

Report: June 24, 1944
Narrator: Sherwood L. Kelly, S./Sgt.

I was riding as tailgunner in 7A, the #3 plane in our box. 7C, A/C#43-27656, was in the #2 position. As we were making the run on the target, the flak was thick and accurate. Looking toward 7C, I noticed that the turret-gunner was on fire and that there was fire all over the turret. Then the plane pulled away from the formation with smoke trailing out behind. One chute came out of the plane, apparently from the rear hatch at the bottom of the plane. Then it looked as if the gas tank on the right wing exploded; but the wing stayed on as the plane went into a dive. I looked away for about 10 seconds and then followed it down until it crashed into the side of a mountain where it burst into one big ball of fire which spread over a large area.

Comments: S/Sgt. Kelly clearly saw Obravatz escape from the rear hatch. He apparently did not see Ahlstrom, Dombrowski, or George, who jumped from the forward hatch.

Report written upon Ed Dombrowski's return to the 487th Squadron about 6 weeks after being shot down on June 22, 1944:

Report: Aug. 3, 1944

Dombrowski witnessed Tail Gunner bail out and saw another chute which, according to the doctor who treated Dombrowski's wounds, was that of Co-Pilot, Lt. George.

On June 29, 1944, Dombrowski was informed by Partisani* that a body with unopened chute had been found in the vicinity and was shown the identification belonging to Sgt. Ahlstrom. Ahlstrom had been given proper burial and headstone placed on the grave.

Partisani stated to Dombrowski that two skulls had been found in the remains of the aircraft.

* Italian Partisans - resistance fighters.

Comments: there was confusion regarding my father's status. The doctor referred to in the report saw George Obravatz, not Harry George. In that area of Italy, surnames and given names were reversed. If George Obravatz gave his correct name in that order, the doctor would have believed that George was his surname and probably referred to him as Tenente (Lt.) George. My father was not seen by a doctor.

Later report filed by Ed Dombrowski:

Report: Sept. 1, 1944
Narrator: Edward P. Dombrowski

Known Information: Italian civilians informed me of two skulls found with the wreckage of the plane and at least a dozen people confirmed this. S./Sgt. Ahlstrom's body with identification was found by these same civilians. This identification was turned over to me. He is buried in the vicinity of Borgo San Lorenzo. A civilian doctor who came into the mountains to treat my wounds told me of a Lt. George whom he had treated for third degree burns. Lt. George was brought to him by German sentries. Besides remembering his name, the description was perfect. I believe Sgt. Kaplan bailed out before I did.

Comments: the doctor was clearly confused re. George Obravatz and Harry George. Dombrowski was also unclear as to whom escaped from the rear of the plane: Obravatz or Kaplan. Obravatz escaped. Kaplan was killed.

My next problem was coming up fast -- I was getting close to the ground and there was nothing but trees -- tall pine trees. I tried to think of what I was supposed to do and could remember nothing. No one ever practiced tree landings anyway.

When you're coming down in trees, you instinctively cover two things -- your crotch and your eyes -- and for damn good reason too, I might add! Just ask your mother.

My mother, Margie, who was also listening to my father's re-telling of his story, knew her cue only too well:

"Now, stop it, Harry! You're embarrassing me!" she interjected in her best modest-maiden tone. "But I am awfully glad your instincts were good -- caring for a *blind* man for all of these years would have been tough, even for a nurse."

We all got a laugh out of that one. My father loved a good retort although he preferred ones that were not at his expense, but Mom had done well with that one and it gave him time to catch his breath. Talking about "that day" still gave him the shakes.

I slid down through the huge pine trees and luckily reached the ground -- with all crucial parts in tact and operating.

"Yes, dear," my mother interjected again, "we've already established that!"

I hit some big branches, but my crotch and eyes were OK. I stood up. My right foot was jammed, but I could walk. That was enough at the moment.

I pulled the chute down out of the trees. I tried to bury it quickly digging in the soft forest ground like a dog and then covering it in much the same way -- first with dirt and then brush -- looking around the entire time to see if anyone -- especially any Germans -- were coming. I then took to the mountain like a mad man – we'd been told that the Germans weren't taking prisoners and I was not about to get shot behind their lines. I just ran and ran and ran.

I guess I was lucky that my chute hadn't opened earlier. I was only in the air for a couple of minutes - hardly enough time for any nearby Germans to get to me. Dombrowski and Obravatz, who had opened their chutes much higher, were captured as soon as they landed or shortly thereafter. But even if the Germans weren't waiting for me when I landed, I knew that they would be after me immediately and I had to get away.

The mountain was steep but entirely wooded. The underbrush was thick. While that made my going difficult at times, it also meant that it would be difficult for the Germans too -- and it would be dark before too long. All I had to do was make it until then -- until dark. Then I would be safe -- at least until morning.

I made it high up on the mountain and, as the darkness came, I was thankful - thankful I was alive, thankful it was summer, and thankful for the trees and the mountain. I was about two hundred miles behind enemy lines, in a foreign country, and unable to speak or understand the language, but I was alive and except for two grazes from our ammunition, some minor burns, and a jammed foot, I was in pretty good shape.

I thought about your mother back home; I had thought of her briefly just after I left the plane. My whole life didn't flash before me -- just her -- and I was damn thankful for her as well. She was someone real and wonderful for me to strive to get home to -- and I would get home to her. And then it dawned on me that she was going to get a rather awful message soon -- an MIA telegram. It was going to get tough on her as well.

My mother interrupted him again:

"That telegram was odd -- but also somewhat anti-climatic. You see, at precisely 1:20 our time on the 22nd -- which was 7:20 PM Italian time, I was walking with another nurse, Peg Ballentine, from one floor of the hospital where I worked to another. I got dizzy and faint -- and knew something had happened to Harry. I didn't know what -- just that something bad had happened. I told Peg. She didn't laugh or comment, but just made a note of the date and time, then she told me to get moving. We had work to do."

My father briefly commented:

I neither believed nor disbelieved your mother's premonition. Those things are beyond my comprehension. That was your mother's reality -- but just as valid as mine, even if I don't understand it.

My mother then continued her account of receiving the M.I.A. telegram:

"But when the telegram came," my mother continued, "the Western Union man wouldn't give it to me. He had been told to deliver it to Mrs. George at the hospital, but when he found me, he told me that he wouldn't give it to me -- he knew Mrs. George and I wasn't her."

"He knew what the telegram said and was looking for your father's mother, Elsie -- someone he had known years ago but didn't know had since died."

"I was furious! Telegrams did not bring good news and I already had this feeling that something bad had happened. I wanted to know and I wanted to know right then! After he left, I rushed down to your Uncle Walt's office and told him what had happened. I was shaking like a leaf! Walt was a World War I vet and knew everyone in town. He was also in charge of the Civil Defense effort. He could get the telegram."

"Walt walked me over to the Western Union office and got the telegram. Your father was MIA, Missing In Action -- as of June 22nd. I was crushed. And I cried. Nothing prepares you for that -- nothing! Not even premonitions."

"Walt stayed with me for several hours. He was upset too. He had served in WW I and knew what war was. He didn't want to lose his youngest brother to this one."

My father continued:

I was scared. I didn't know what tomorrow would bring and I didn't have a gun. What I did know was that whatever tomorrow brought, it wouldn't be as horrifying as June 22nd had been.

I had thought after my first mission -- a bombing run over the Gustav Line near Monte Cassino and a real baptism of fire -- that I realized what war was -- that they were shooting at ME. But on June 22nd, I really understood what war was. As necessary as it was to fight and defeat the Nazis, war was the random and brutal death of good people and it was sheer terror. It wasn't Hell; it was far worse!

Plate 1

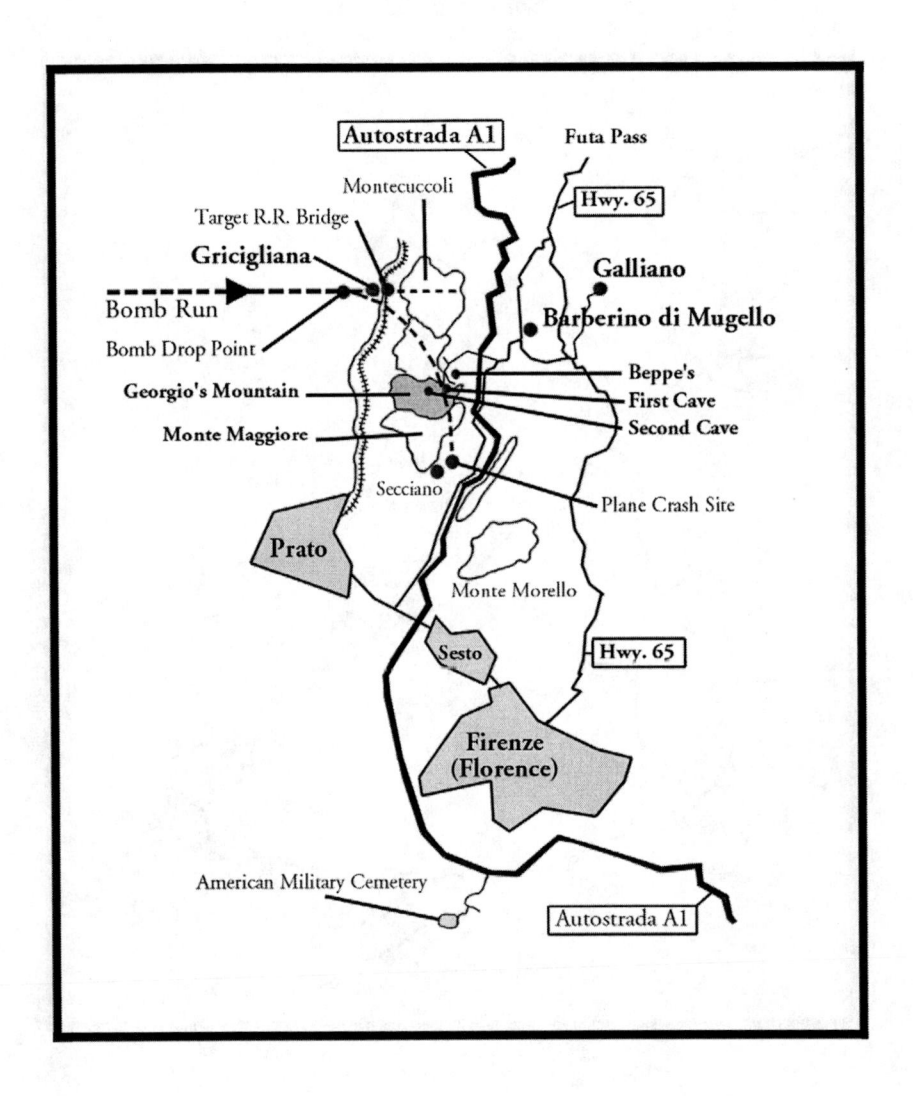

Area Map / Story Locations

Plate 2

Italy
Principal Cities, Bombing Missions

Plate 3

B-25 Schematic Diagram

North American B-25 Mitchell Medium Bomber

J Model

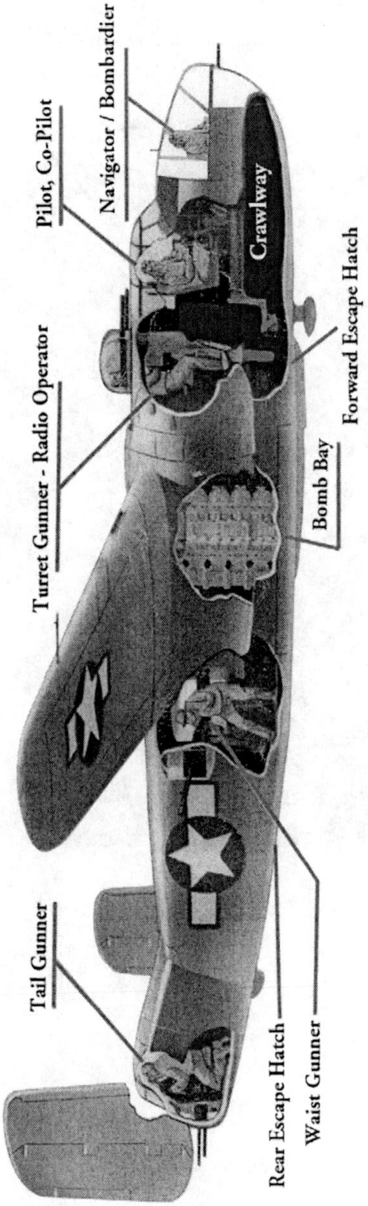

- Pilot, Co-Pilot
- Navigator / Bombardier
- Crawway
- Forward Escape Hatch
- Turret Gunner - Radio Operator
- Bomb Bay
- Tail Gunner
- Rear Escape Hatch
- Waist Gunner

Plate 4

June 22, 1944

Gricigliana Mission Photo

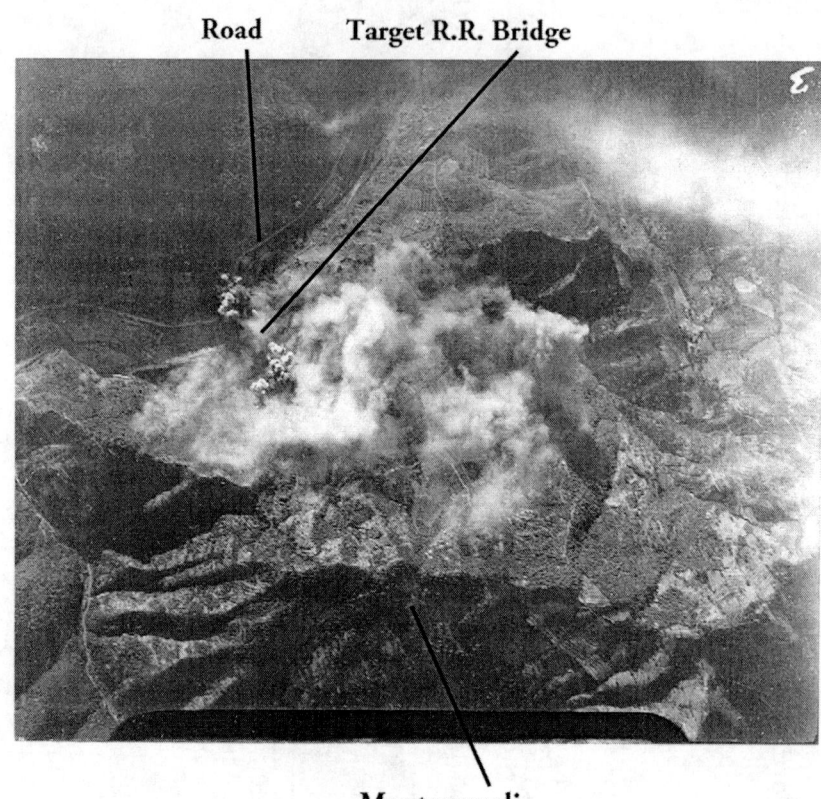

Plate 5

June 22, 1944

7C, The McKinley Jr. High, Going Down

Plate 6

WESTERN UNION

RXPB45 44 GOVT = WUX WASHINGTON DC JUL 6 827A

MRS MARGARET E GEORGE =

547 OLIVE ST CS =

THE SECRETARY OF WAR DESIRES ME TO EXPRESS HIS DEEP REGRET THAT YOUR HUSBAND SECOND LIEUTENANT HARRY D GEORGE HAS BEEN REPORTED MISSING IN ACTION SINCE TWENTY TWO JUNE OVER ITALY IF FURTHER DETAILS OR OTHER INFORMATION ARE RECEIVED YOU WILL BE PROMPTLY NOTIFIED =

ULIO THE ADJUTANT GENERAL.

JUL 6 837A

Lieut. George Missing Upon Bombing Raid

Well Known Local Young Man Overseas Six Weeks

Word was received here today that Lt. Harry D. George, Coatesville, is missing in action in a bombing mission over Italy. A telegram from the War Department conveyed the news he has been missing since June 22.

The telegram was received by his wife, Margaret George, a nurse at Coatesville hospital, but gave no further details. It set forth further information will be forwarded when received at Washington.

Lieutenant George was pilot of a Mitchell bomber.

A son of the late Fred George, he is well known here. He received his pilot wings last February at an air field in the west and spent a leave here with relatives before flying across the Atlantic for combat duty.

He has been overseas about six weeks.

July 6, 1944

Word Reaches Home

HERE'S hoping that Lieut. Harry D. George, Coatesville, pilot of a Mitchell bomber, reported missing in action over Italy, turns up safely some place. He is about as clean-cut a young man you could possibly meet anywhere and deserved a better fate than to vanish after being overseas only six weeks.

Plate 7

Georgio At Caves
(June, 1944)

At First Cave

At Second Cave

Plate 8

Georgio Italiano!

Plate 9

Four Friends

Renzo Fantoni   Georgio

Guiseppe 'Beppe' Ferri   Nello Niccoli

Plate 10

The Ferri Family

Dina, Graziella, Beppe

Bruna, Lina

Gino

Georgio

Signore Ferri   Uncle Angelino

Plate 11

Georgio and Friends

Danilo, Emilio, Georgio, Bruno, Piero
Lindo and Doriana Ferri, Vasco, Gino, Beppe and Gino Ferri
Vasco, Piero Fantoni, Nello Niccoli

Fernanda Fantoni, Georgio, Bruna Ferri, Rina, Luciana
Dina Ferri
Julia & Doriana Ferri, Dina Niccoli, Cesira
Graziella and Lina Ferri, Franca Fantoni, Bruna Ferri

Plate 12

September 21, 1944
The Good News Reaches Home

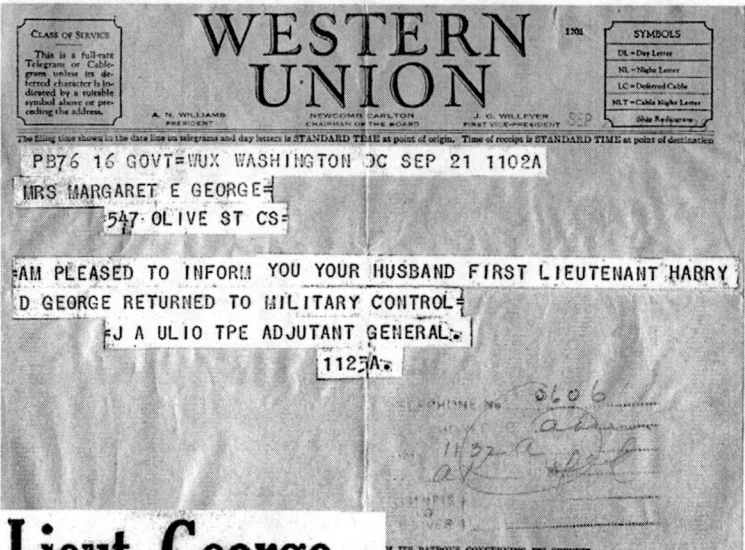

WESTERN UNION

PB76 16 GOVT=WUX WASHINGTON DC SEP 21 1102A
MRS MARGARET E GEORGE=
547 OLIVE ST CS=

AM PLEASED TO INFORM YOU YOUR HUSBAND FIRST LIEUTENANT HARRY D GEORGE RETURNED TO MILITARY CONTROL=
J A ULIO TPE ADJUTANT GENERAL.
1125A.

Lieut. George, Long Missing, Reported Safe

Local Pilot Back With Military In Italy

"Am pleased to inform you that your husband, First Lieutenant Harry D. George, has returned to military control."

This telegram, signed by the Adjutant General, climaxed weeks of anxiety for Mrs. Margaret George, who was notified on last July sixth that her pilot husband was missing after a bomber raid over Italy.

Lt. George

Lt. George had been officially listed "missing in action" since June 22, exactly one month after he landed in Corsica to begin operations over Europe. No word has ever been received as to the number of missions Lt. George has flown. His wife says that he never mentioned his flights in letters to her, saying merely that he had been "very busy."

A letter which Mrs. George received from her husband's commanding officer the first of August described the mission from which Lt. George failed to return. The letter said that the B-25 which he piloted had suffered a direct hit over Italy, but that it had gone down under control and a parachute dropped from it. Other letters from his fellow officers gave encouraging information, and his wife continued to hope for his safety although official word did not come through until yesterday.

Lt. George, a son of the late Fred George, left for overseas duty last May. He had been overseas only six weeks when the telegram which reported him missing was received. His wife is a nurse at the Coatesville hospital.

Plate 13

Lieut. George, An Army Nurse, Dies In Crash

December 29, 1944

Tragic News Sent Kin Here Of Airplane Tragedy

ON WAY HOME

Young Woman In Service Long Time In Near East

Miss Rebecca L. George, Coatesville, an Army nurse, in the service for three years, much of which time was spent in the Near East, was killed in an airplane crash in Africa last Friday, December 29.

Stunning news of this tragedy was received here late yesterday in a telegram from the War Department at Washington, D. C.

Miss George is believed to have been on her way home for a furlough when the accident occurred. She had intimated in letters to relatives she expected to be able to spend a vacation here in the near future.

The telegram to her brother, French S. George, this city, read:

"The Secretary of War asks that I assure you of his deep sympathy in the loss of your sister, Second Lieutenant Rebecca L. George. Report received says she was killed December 29 in Africa in an airplane crash. (Signed Dunlop, Acting Adjutant General."

While serving at different U. S. army hospitals in the Near East Lieut. George had met several Coatesville service men and women, one of whom in a letter received a few days ago said she was awaiting travel orders for a furlough back home.

Lieut. George's half-brother, Lieut. Harry George, had a miraculous escape from death or capture several months ago when his bomber was shot down behind German lines in Italy. Although in a precarious predicament for seventy-eight days, he succeeded in getting back to American lines, after which he was given a furlough to his home here. A few weeks ago he, was reassigned for duty as an instructor.

Miss George has another half-brother, Fred George, who resides at Claymont, Del., and a step-brother, Walter Carlin, Coatesville.

Lieut. George was born and raised in Coatesville. She was a graduate of Coatesville high school and the nurses' training school of the Lancaster General hospital.

Beck

RECALLING the recent receipt of word that Lieut. Rebecca L. George lost her life in an airplane accident somewhere in Africa; imagine the terrific shock when her best friend, another Army nurse, picked up a newspaper and read about it while traveling by train from Florida to her home in New England. The two had worked together in India and received furloughs at the same time to come back home. By some queer twist of fate the friend departed by plane one day earlier than Miss George.

ALL this revives what our best pal told us whilst on a furlough: "Dad when my number comes up there will be nothing I can do about it." There wasn't.

—Word was received Lieut. Rebecca L. George, U. S. Army nurse, of Coatesville, was killed in airplane crash in Africa while returning from India.

FOR the kind of news that sears the heart you will get none more shocking than that conveyed by a War Department telegram telling of the death in an airplane crash of Lieut. Rebecca L. George, an Army nurse from Coatesville. For three long years she had used her professional skill to minister unto the sick, the wounded and the dying of our service men. Doubtless due to her efforts and those of associates many lives were saved. Came the time when the richly deserved furlough papers reached her in far-off India followed by travel orders by air. One week ago today (but for the accident she would be home here today with her loved ones and friends) the plane crashed somewhere in Africa, costing her life. She gave her all for the nation she loved. No finer tribute than that could be put into words.

Plate 14

Reunion in 1969 - The Ferris

Beppe and Georgio

Beppe, Margie, Georgio, and Dina

Plate 15

1969 Reunion - The Niccolis

Nello and Georgio

Niccoli Family Party For Georgio:
Second Row: Beppe, Nello, Margie, Dina, Mario

Plate 16

Reunion in 1969 - The Fantonis

Georgio, Renzo, Fernanda, Margie

Piero Fantoni in doorway.

Plate 17

Reunion in 1969

Back At The First Cave

Nello, Georgio, and Beppe

Plate 18

1969 Reunion - At The Padrone's

Nello, Georgio, Beppe, Alphonso Manelli - The Padrone

American Military Overseas Cemeteries

Cemetery	War	Location	Country	Burials	Missing
Europe:					
Aisne Marne	WWI	South Of Belleau	France	2,289	1,060
Ardennes	WWII	Southwest of Liege	Belgium	5,328	462
Brittany	WWII	1.5 miles SE of St. James	France	4,410	498
Brookwood	WWI	25 miles South of London	England	468	563
Cambridge	WWII	3 miles West of Cambridge	England	3,812	5,126
Epinal	WWII	4 miles South of Epinal	France	5,255	424
Flanders Field	WWI	near Waregem	Belgium	368	43
Florence	WWII	7.5 miles South of Florence	Italy	4,402	1,409
Henri-Chapelle	WWII	Northeast of Henri-Chapelle	Belgium	7,989	450
Lorraine	WWII	Avold	France	10,489	444
Luxembourg	WWII	Luxembourg City (incl. Gen'l Patton)	Luxembourg	5,076	371
Meuse-Argonne	WWI	Romagne-sous-Montfaucon	France	14,246	954
Netherlands	WWII	Margraten	Netherlands	8,302	1,723
Normandy	WWII	Omaha Beach	France	9,387	1,557
Oise-Aisne	WWI	1.5 miles East of Fere-en-Tardenois,	France	6,012	241
Rhone	WWII	Draguigan	France	861	294
St. Michiel	WWI	Southeast of Verdun	France	4,153	284
Sicily-Rome	WWII	30 miles South of Rome	Italy	7,861	3,095
Somme	WWI	Bony	France	1,844	333
Sunresnes	WWI, WWII	Western City Limits of Paris	France	1,591	974
Other:					
Corozal	WWI	Panama City	Panama	5,144	
Manila	WWII	Manila	Philippines	17,206	36,282
Mexico City	Mex. War	Mexico City	Mexico	750	
North Africa	WWII	Carthage	Tunisia	2,841	3,724
TOTAL				130,084	60,311

Plate 19

Chapter Twelve
Georgio Italiano

Giuseppe Ferri, known affectionately as Beppe, and Nello Niccoli were both out in the garden the evening of June 22, 1944 and saw and heard our bombers. They heard the bombs hit on the other side of Montecuccoli, saw our plane go down and crash near Secciano, saw Ahlstrom plummet like a torch from the plane, saw the two chutes disappear on the other side of the mountain, and saw my chute come down on their side of the mountain only about a mile away.

They knew better than to go chasing after a downed airman right away. They could be shot -- either by the American or by the Germans who were certain to be after him. Instead, they waited awhile, went and located the partially buried parachute and buried it well. They then went to see the Padrone who owned the land they farmed and for whom they worked. Renzo Fantoni, a friend of the Padrone's who was living with them for the duration, went with them.

Nello was excited. There was an American in their area. Many of his friends from his hometown in Southern Italy had emigrated to America. He felt a kinship with America and wanted to help the American. Beppe was more reserved. He hated the Germans. They were brutal. They had overrun his country, taxed his farm production at 100 per cent, sometimes occupied their houses, took their livestock, and could not be trusted. They were neither civil nor human. He would help the American. Americans were decent people. They were fighting the Germans and trying to drive them from Italy. The Americans were his allies. He would help the American, but he would be quiet about it.

Renzo had served in the Italian Army before its collapse. He understood the fascist mentality. The Italian version of it was benign by comparison to the German. Mussolini made the trains run on time. The Germans were different. Harsh. He didn't like them and he liked Americans. He wanted to help the American, but his friend, the Padrone, and his assets would have to be kept safe – for all of their sakes.

They reached the Padrone's villa. The Padrone was a dignified and wealthy man. He was also very decent as far as Padrones went, but he had a huge economic interest at stake. He would not do anything to cause the Germans to take his land and wealth away. Beppe was not sure that he should be told at all, but Renzo was the Padrone's friend and there was no stopping Nello. The Padrone was going to know one way or the other and better to talk to him now than later.

Nello did the talking at first. He was excited. He told the Padrone about the downed American flier who was very near to their farmhouse. He thought that they should help him. Renzo agreed. The Padrone listened and thought. He knew that the tide of the war was turning. The Italian fascist government had already collapsed and the Germans were in control. He knew that they wouldn't upset things too much right now, but if they won, his wealth would likely be confiscated by the Third Reich.

He pondered long and hard about what to do. Then he asked Beppe what he thought. Beppe, too, was a dignified man. He features were strong despite his thin frame. Although a tenant farmer, Beppe was respected everywhere. He was a natural leader. His opinions were always measured, always thoughtful, and always balanced. Whenever he spoke on an issue, everyone listened. He made sense -- good sense.

Beppe thought that the American should be helped, it was the right thing to do. But he should be helped clandestinely and by only a very limited group of people, especially since the Germans' local headquarters were located in the church just a half mile from their farmhouse -- and the American should certainly not have any contact with the Padrone. Renzo agreed.

There were three families living in Beppe's house. They could take care of the American -- but on the mountain, not on the farm. There were caves that could be used for hiding. They could take food to him at night. The men were hunters and they all could negotiate the mountain very well at night. They would admit to no one what they were doing. The Padrone agreed and it was done.

As Beppe, Nello, and Renzo left to walk back to their house, they discussed readying a cave which was close to the farmhouse. They would take some straw up for a bed first thing in the morning. They had often talked about what they would do if an American flyer were shot down. Now all of their what-if conversations were coming to reality.

Their wives would have to know as well. There might be times when the men could not be seen going toward the mountain and their wives would have to take him food. They could take some of their animals and tie them to trees for protection from the air strikes so that they could claim to be taking food to their livestock if they were caught. Yes, that would work.

Now, they just had to contact the American. That too could be dangerous. He would be armed, very scared, and very suspicious. He might shoot them, but no...an American would not shoot an Italian farmer.

They arrived home and told their wives about their discussion with the Padrone. They went to bed with nervous excitement. They weren't in the war as combatants -- it had always seemed like folly to them -- but now that the war had come to them they would participate.

Daylight came early -- too early. I hadn't slept much. As darkness had set in the night before, I found a clump of bushes high up on the mountain to curl up under for the night. I pushed some leaves and pine needles together as a bed and crawled underneath making sure that the clump of bushes was big enough and thick enough to hide me.

The darkness had been total. The trees were tall and thick and blocked out many of the stars. The bushes were thicker yet. I wanted to be able to see something to keep my bearings, but it was difficult. I tried to think and could not do so clearly. I knew I had to sleep because the Germans would be after me at first light. I didn't want to sleep because that meant losing control and losing safety. Finally, after listening to the sounds of the forest, animal footsteps which sounded heavy and Germanic, and keeping one eye open for what seemed like hours, I drifted off to sleep.

The morning light woke all the birds, the roosters on the farm, and me. I opened my eyes with a start. This was real! This was happening! It was not a dream. I was alone behind the lines and had no way to get any food and I was getting hungry. I listened intently for several minutes before moving and, after hearing no dangerous sounds, crawled out from under the bushes and stood up. Every action required careful thought and courage -- even just standing up.

The mountain was very high, probably a couple thousand feet. The trees were thick and there were two other mountains close by. I had a lot of cover. I tried looking down into the valley. I was a long way from any houses. I would be able to hear someone coming -- well, I thought I would be able to hear them. I couldn't be sure.

I had to relieve myself -- badly. I stood there and thought about it. There was no margin for error here -- even in routine bodily functions. A wet spot on the ground would be a give-away. And it shouldn't be too close to where I was. What was I going to do that day? What could I do? Should I move or stay put? There really wasn't too much I could do. Daytime was dangerous and the Germans would surely send a patrol or two out looking for me. I would stay put and hide under my bushes. I looked at them again. Could I be seen under there? No. They were big and thick, but then again wouldn't the Germans look under there? Or just fire a few shots into them? But where could I run? Everywhere I could think of there would be more Germans -- except here on the mountain. I would have to risk relying on the bushes...and would have to relieve myself somewhere else.

I slowly moved away from the clump of bushes. I kept them in sight and constantly scanned everything for any sign of movement. I got about 50 feet away. That was far enough. I thought about relieving myself again. I didn't want a pool. I remembered driving to West Chester, Pa. with Margie when we were setting up our apartment shortly before we were married. It was winter. The ground was snow-covered and I got caught short along Creek Road. I got out of the car and in my best smart-ass mode, wrote my name in the snow -- even dotting the "i" in my middle name. I proudly called for Margie to get out of the car to look at my handiwork.

She was half amused and half disgusted, but broke out laughing when I started a dissertation on all the years it had taken me to cultivate and perfect my pee-writing skill -- especially the ability to dot "i"s without dribbling.

"Harry can expostulate on anything," my mother interjected, "and the more absurd it is, the more seriously he expounds on it."

I chuckled silently at that memory while I was standing there debating on how best to relieve myself. Writing my name here would not be at all smart, but spraying things around would be. There was still a lot of dew on the plants and spray would be indistinguishable from it. So I sprayed. And then went back to my bushes.

The more I thought about it, the more I realized that I could not go anywhere during the day. I am tall and would be easily visible. Going over the mountain to the west would take me toward the coast but also into the German nest around the bridge. Going north was pure folly -- that was deeper into German territory. Going south was feasible. That was the direction back to the American troops. There was an even higher mountain to the South and, I wasn't sure about this, but the outskirts of Florence couldn't be too far. But the Germans were heavily entrenched around Florence. South would have to wait. I needed to find sustenance first.

That left east. There were some farm houses and I could see a small village down in the bottom of the valley. I could possibly sneak down to one of the farm houses. The Italians at home in Coatesville, PA all had gardens. In fact, they were fanatical about their gardens. They must have brought that custom with them and there would likely be gardens near the houses. But evening would be better. I would have the fading light and the shadow of the mountain to my advantage. In short, the only thing it made sense to do was to stay put all day under my clump of bushes.

While I wanted to simply sit there and keep watch all day, it made more sense to hide. I crawled back under the bushes and pulled myself as close together in a ball as I could. It was going to be a long day, but I was thinking clearly now. I felt good about my assessment of the situation.

I went over things a million times in the next hour or so. I wound my watch. I would need to pay close attention to time. I had gotten up at 0530 and the sun was already up. What time did the sun go down yesterday? I didn't remember, not precisely anyway. I had checked my watch too much and remembered too many different times. Sometime around eight o'clock I thought. Finally, and unintentionally, I drifted back to sleep.

Then I heard something and opened my eyes with a start. I didn't like what I saw -- four pairs of German jack boots standing beside the bush. Had they seen me? We'd been told that the Germans were no longer taking prisoners of war. Were they just waiting for me to stir to kill me? I saw the barrels of their rifles pointing toward the ground. They had sent a patrol looking for me. I was in deep trouble.

My heart was beating heavily, so heavily that I could hear and feel every beat like it was a jackhammer in my chest. Surely, even the Germans could hear it too! I couldn't move. Where were my legs? Were they still pulled up or had I extended them in my sleep? I tried to feel where they were without moving them. They were still curled up. Thank God for that.

The Germans were talking. I couldn't fathom a word of what they were saying. Why hadn't I paid more attention in German Class in high school? That would have paid off now even if I never heard another word of it. They were saying something and all turned to look somewhere. I had to sneeze. I couldn't sneeze. I couldn't even risk moving my hand up to stop it. They might hear that. I willed that sneeze away. My life depended on not sneezing and I was not going to do it. Period. I didn't.

They turned again and one started to walk away. The others followed. The last one poked his rifle into the bush -- just one final check. I was looking up the barrel from 18 inches away, but the German pulled it back and moved on with the others. The bushes had worked and I had been deep enough in them. I had not been seen.

I listened with acuity to the sounds of Germans scouring the mountain. They got farther and farther away. My heart was still pounding in my chest, but it gradually calmed down. I didn't move for an hour, but I was not going to doze off again. That was too goddamned close!

I finally moved and looked at my watch. It was 0730 -- almost time for take-off back on Corsica for the morning mission. In another hour the Squadron might be back. If we missed the bridge at Gricigliana yesterday, we would keep coming back until we got it -- maybe not every day, but almost. In an hour, I would listen for the planes. I wanted to hear them. I wanted some connection with America. I wanted to hear the sweet roar of B-25's again. Then again, I hoped that we had gotten the target. Casey, Kaplan, and Ahlstrom had to have died for something -- some success, some meaning. It would be better if I didn't hear the planes. What was I going to do? My plan was sound. I would stay put until evening. I just had to stay under the bushes all day.

Shots! I heard gunshots! What was going on? Whom or what were the Germans shooting at? Could Dombrowski or Obravatz have come over the mountain? No, there was little likelihood of that. Were the Germans shooting Italian civilians? That was certainly possible.

When I arrived on Corsica, I had no particular grudge with Germans. I knew that we had to fight and defeat the Nazis, but America was a mixing bowl of ethnic groups. There were many people of German heritage there and they seemed as American as any of the others. Hell, Aunt Mary had even tried to tell me that the George family had come to America in the 1740's from Germany. Or was it England? I didn't remember. But I didn't dislike anyone just because of the country their family came from.

My ambivalence toward the Germans had changed after my first mission. I had realized that they -- the Germans -- were shooting at ME! Now they were just shooting at innocent Italians. It had to be. We were 200 miles behind the lines. What else could they be shooting at? As I would later learn, it probably was Italians - but ones who had taken to the hills in fear of the Germans.

The shots stopped and there was silence.

Nothing else happened on June 23rd. My hunger and thirst grew, but I willed them away at least for the time being. I listened. I heard the sounds of the valley -- the German heavy equipment moving down the roads, a few cars, and what sounded like a tractor now and then. I heard the birds singing in the trees. They annoyed me. This wasn't a picnic. This was war! Birds weren't needed here! And their occasional loud shrieks were startling.

Finally, the shadows started making their way down the eastern side of the mountain. It would be dusk soon. I hadn't heard any military sounds for several hours. There had been no planes all day. That was good -- we had hit the bridge yesterday and the Squadron was going after other targets. I silently wished them well and hoped that there wasn't any flak. God, that stuff was insidious. I remembered the name of our tent back on Corsica, "Flak Happy." We'd change that for sure if I got back!

I decided to crawl out and stand up. I listened first. Nothing. It was time.

I crawled slowly out -- listening after each movement for some reaction.

There were none. I crouched. I looked around. Still nothing. Finally, I stood. Geez, just standing up felt good. We take so much for granted I thought. I would never have imagined feeling such a thrill in just standing up. But I did. It was glorious!

The valley looked peaceful. It was beautiful actually. There were mountains and hills all around -- with beautiful trees, lovely fields, pretty farm houses and a lovely village nestled among the small hills in the valley. It was time now to try and find some food and water. My hunger and thirst were getting stronger and I would need some light to get back up the mountain. It was simply too dark at night to see anything. Yes, it was time.

I started making my way down the mountain holding onto trees and tree limbs as I went. The mountain was very steep and the soil was soft forest soil. The footing was not firm. After moving about 50 feet, I came upon what appeared to be a path. That was not good. It was too close to my bushes. Would I be able to find my bushes again? I looked around for landmarks. There weren't any that I could make out. A forest is a forest. Well, I had to eat. I needed water. I would just have to risk it.

But what was this path? I looked at it. There were too many stones in it for it to be a footpath. I followed it with my eyes and noticed a pattern. It joined with another one and then twisted and turned. I looked at where it came from above me. Same thing. It was a path formed by rainwater running off the mountain. That was a revelation. It had to end in a stream somewhere. Water! And I was getting desperately thirsty. And I might be able to use the run-off path to get back up to my bushes. Things were definitely looking up.

I slowly began walking down it. The ground was more firm. I didn't need to hold onto the trees anymore. I could actually walk.

I followed it down into a crevice between my mountain and the one next to it and there was a tiny stream there. It was shallow, but I cupped my hands and drank the crystal clear water...and drank and drank. I felt good. I could survive on my own.

My thirst was satiated, but the hunger was still there. I looked around. It looked like there was an old dirt road leading up to the stream a little way farther down. I didn't want to be on a road of any kind, but if I followed it from above, where there are roads, there are houses and gardens. Now I just had to decide on the timing.

I decided that tomorrow would be a better day for foraging for food. I was safe and had gotten the water I needed. That was enough -- and there was still enough light for me to find my way back to my bushes.

I went back to my lair and went to sleep.

The second morning, my hunger was getting acute and my thirst was returning. I was up at 0530 again, but by 0800 am there was still no evidence of any patrols. I decided to return to the stream and at least get some more water in my stomach.

I followed the run-off paths back down to the stream and got water. I could make out some houses and what I thought was a garden alongside the ravine that the stream had carved in the mountainside. I stood there debating whether to try to get some food from the garden in the daylight or whether to try and wait it out 'til evening. I was getting incredibly hungry and didn't know if I could wait that long.

I didn't get a chance to make that decision. There walking along the old dirt road next to a high stone retaining wall was a short, Italian-looking guy dressed like a farmer. Had he seen me yet? The Italian started waving his hands above his head. He had seen me. What to do? Run? I still had a chance at disappearing into the brush on the mountain. Should I risk it? The Italian guy was now smiling and waving and walking toward me even faster.

Every instinct told me to run and run fast. But the guy was clearly trying to be friendly and didn't look armed. And how many more days could I survive Germans within a couple feet of me? How many more times could I will away a sneeze? I had to make a decision and make it on the spot. I did. I decided to risk it. I was much bigger than this guy and could overpower him if I had to.

"Americano?" Nello asked.

I didn't know a word of Italian, but I did understand that. I shook my head 'yes.'

"Mi amico!" Nello responded. "Amico" I understood and smiled.

We got closer. Nello signaled for me to come with him. Both of us were very tense and didn't want to make any threatening moves.

Nello didn't head back down the road. That would have been cause for some concern. He headed a little up from the creek bed and along the side of the mountain. I followed.

After several minutes, Nello stopped. He pointed to a cave opening. I felt very good. This guy actually was going to help me. I moved up closer to Nello and looked in. This was almost too good to be true. Nello pointed to his chest and said, "Nello. Niccoli Nello." He then pointed to me. I said my full name - "Harry George." "Ah, Georgio!", Nello responded instantly. In that part of Italy, the names are reversed -- family name first, given name, second. Thus, I became 'Georgio.'

"Nello - Georgio" he said pointing to each of us. I was now 'Georgio' -- an American-Italian (rather than vice versa).

With that, Nello motioned for me to go into the cave and started talking a mile a minute. He was quite an animated guy and clearly was very friendly. Finally, Nello started making hand motions which indicated eating.

"Mangiare!" Nello said.

I, now 'Georgio' and not 'Harry,' shook my head 'Yes.' I mimicked his eating motions, and repeated, "mangiare!"

I was hungry. Very hungry. It had been almost two days since I had eaten and even that was only a light lunch of goddamned army food.

Agreement having been reached, Nello started talking fast again and finally started to move away. I made the eating motions and said, "mangiare" again and thought Nello understood -- Nello was to go for food. He repeated "mangiare" and nodded 'Yes.' So did I - one last time.

I sat and watched as Nello bounded away through the woods and then back down the dirt road. Could I trust this guy? Should I wait there or hide?

What if Nello came back with Germans or if they followed him? I had to hide. I would hide close-by and watch. Maybe, just maybe, I had lucked out and found a friendly Italian.

I climbed above the cave and found another good clump of bushes. I was starting to like bushes immensely. I had always disliked them before -- they always seemed to be in the wrong places and were a pain in the ass in the yard. They had to be trimmed and always seemed to devour baseballs when I was a kid. Now they were good. They gave me needed cover.

It wasn't long before I heard footsteps and branches cracking. I saw Nello. He had what looked like a long loaf of Italian bread sticking out of a burlap bag. There was also someone else with him. That made me very nervous. I didn't want my whereabouts broadcast and certainly not that soon. I watched. The other guy was calm -- not exuberant like Nello. As they got closer, I saw his face. It was a good face. A serious face.

I looked behind them. There was no one. No Germans.

Nello and the other guy got to the cave and there was no 'Georgio.' Nello was crestfallen. The other guy motioned to Nello to be quiet. I liked that. They looked around, looked behind them. The new guy said something to Nello and they both found a place to sit down -- but in clear view. I liked this guy. He was cautious and thoughtful. This was a guy I could trust.

I came out of my new clump of bushes and started down toward them. Nello jumped up and the new guy quickly grabbed him and indicated for him to be quiet. I definitely liked this guy. I walked down to them. More pointing -- 'Nello,' 'Georgio,' and the new guy -- 'Beppe.'

They handed me the burlap bag. I looked in it -- a loaf of bread, a salami and a bottle of wine. Geez, not only was I going to get fed, I was going to have a full meal complete with wine. These guys were quite all right with me!

Beppe motioned for me to follow him into the cave. He bent over. The ceiling was barely four feet high. Beppe lit a match and showed me the cave. The floor sloped gently downward and then in the back, about 10 feet from the opening, there was a ledge that was high up and not visible from the front - a perfect hiding place. Not only that, there was a bed of straw nicely and thickly spread out on the ledge. I could actually sleep here. They must have made this up for me. That made me feel even more confident.

Few words were said. Beppe motioned that the bread was not only to eat, but also to be used as a pillow -- that was the reason for the burlap sack. Beppe kept saying one word over and over and motioning in a big arc meaning all around.

"Tedeschi. Tedeschi," he said. "Tedeschi malle."

Finally, I got it. 'Tedeschi' meant Germans. They were all around. 'Malle' had to mean something bad. I nodded that I understood.

"Capisce?" Beppe asked.

Ah! That word I knew from playing ball with the Italian kids back home. It meant 'understand?' I understood.

"Capish" I said. "Capish -- Tedeschi (hand motion all around) -- Tedeschi malle."

Beppe smiled. Nello smiled. I smiled.

With that, Nello hugged me. Beppe hugged me. I had never hugged another man before -- it just wasn't done in the States, but it felt good. There was trust there. There was affection there. I felt much, much, better. I felt very, very lucky.

With that, Beppe motioned to Nello that they should leave.

"Domani," Beppe said. "Domani."

I didn't know what it meant, but I agreed. "Domani." "Tomorrow."

I watched them go. Nello was whispering a mile a minute into Beppe's ear. Beppe was listening and nodding -- occasionally making a point with Nello and gesturing emphatically with his finger. The two friends gradually faded into the trees and darkness of the forest.

"My God, what a stroke of luck," I thought. "Unbelievable!"

I bit into the bread. Then the salami. I pulled the partially inserted cork from the wine bottle. Nothing had ever tasted better than that meal. I filled my stomach and then sat on the floor of the cave for a long time wondering why Nello and Beppe were helping me. They had to be putting a lot at risk. What was there for them to gain? Nothing. Nothing at all and a lot to lose. They were just doing it out of human decency. That was almost unfathomable. But it was. It was!

As evening finally set in, I crawled up on the ledge, rested my head on the burlap-covered loaf of bread and fell fast asleep.

Chapter Thirteen
'Sta Sera

"Achtung!" was the first sound I heard on June 25, 1944. I was shocked! I was betrayed! I opened my eyes wide. There was a pair of German jack boots standing right outside the cave entrance.

"Achtung!"

I heard running -- clearly more Germans. Three more sets of boots stopped at the entrance to the cave. Had Nello and Beppe turned me in? Could there something for them in doing that? Were the Germans paying bounties for Americans? Had I been foolish to trust Nello and Beppe? I didn't know. All I knew was that I didn't dare move. It was my first morning all over again.

The Krauts were now facing the cave and talking. Were there footprints outside the cave? I couldn't remember whether the ground had been soft or hard, wet or dry. Maybe it was just another patrol that had stumbled on the cave. Whatever. I would certainly know the answer soon enough. Right now, the Germans weren't coming in. They were just looking. I had to be still.

Noise! There was some noise in the cave. I heard the German rifles snap to position. What was this noise? I hadn't moved. What was it?

I looked toward my feet. There was a squirrel trying to get at something behind my legs. Without thinking, I kicked that goddamned squirrel toward the front of the cave. It hit the ground, saw the Germans, and took off running out of the corner of the cave. The Germans started laughing. They were all set to blow an American to smithereens and all it was a squirrel! They laughed and laughed and laughed as only loud and obnoxious Krauts could do.

I didn't really understand these morning patrols. No enemy is going to wait for the first light of day to do anything. That's just the easiest way to get caught. Evening was when to catch a solitary enemy behind the lines. And even if they were just after me, they had to have figured that I would have been long gone by then. They had complete control over the territory anyway. I could do nothing to them. But they patrolled in the mornings nonetheless.

One of them made some comment and they fired some shots. What were they doing, shooting squirrels? Apparently! They then left as quickly as they had arrived -- probably chasing that squirrel all over the mountain. Oh, they would write it up as chasing an American pilot, but they were simply chasing a squirrel.

I was relieved. Had they come into the cave at all, they would have seen me on the ledge and I would have been shot or captured. But that threat was gone now. I was also relieved that Nello and Beppe had apparently not turned me in. If they had, the Krauts would have known about the back of the cave and found me. Beppe and Nello were trustworthy, but I didn't want to stay in that cave any longer.

I looked at my watch. It was 0630 -- about the same time as the first day's patrol. I remained still for an hour. I wasn't going anywhere in the daylight. I did nibble on some of the bread, but did not leave the ledge.

About 0730, I heard some steps approaching. I listened. They were lighter steps and regular -- and there was only one set.

"Georgio," Beppe whispered into the cave. "Georgio?"

"Beppe?" I whispered in reply and with that Beppe slipped into the cave.

"Vieni con me, ora!" Beppe said. "Tedeschi proxime qui."

I didn't understand a word of it. I didn't like the hand signs Beppe was making signaling me to come with him. I looked at Beppe's face. He was scared. He wouldn't be scared if he had betrayed me. I felt good again -- about Beppe and Nello. They could be trusted. I grabbed the burlap bag, the salami and the bottle of wine and followed Beppe.

Beppe was clearly at home on this mountain. He moved easily and quickly and seemed to know exactly where he was going. He climbed up the mountain occasionally reaching back to give me a hand to get up an over some of the tougher spots and overhangs. Up we went, farther and farther. I thought that we were getting close to where my bushes were, but I couldn't be sure.

Then there was a steep incline and above it what looked like an entrance to another cave. Beppe was taking me to a better hiding place -- away from the paths and concealed much better. I liked and trusted Beppe more each minute.

Beppe pulled me up to the small ledge in front of the cave. This cave didn't have any hidden ledge in the back. It was more like a large crevice in a rock than a cave, but it was deep enough for protection and couldn't be seen into readily. It wasn't perfect, but it was much better than the other one.

Beppe tried to explain something to me in Italian. I couldn't understand any of it. What I knew was that I would stay put in this cave for the day -- or however, long it took to figure out some way to get out of the area and back to the Americans. I hugged Beppe and smiled. Beppe patted me on the back.

"Sta sera," Beppe said.

I didn't know what that meant either, but I trusted Beppe now. Whatever it meant, I believed that it was OK because Beppe was OK.

Beppe said something about Nello. I picked out 'buono' and knew that meant 'good.' I also gathered from the hand signs that Beppe thought Nello was perhaps a bit too talkative. I didn't know whether that meant that Nello had said something to someone who tipped the Germans off, or whether Nello simply was a bit too talkative generally. I figured the latter since it was clear that Nello had said nothing to the Germans or they would have found me that morning.

Anyway, I was pleased and Beppe seemed pleased with the new cave.

"Sta sera," Beppe said again and he started down the mountain.

I sat in the cave looking out and trying to think. What to do next? I had food for at least another couple of days. I could use the wine bottle for water when it was empty -- that I could take care of in the evening. For now, I would just stay put.

I sighed a big sigh of relief. I had been there three days and had two very close calls. At least I was still alive, but I didn't want this every day. I was powerless. I didn't like that feeling. I had always been in control of everything and every situation and now, there was damn little I could do on my own. My sole objective was staying alive.

I knew that sooner or later the Americans would get up to where I was. While the Germans were good and courageous fighters, their factories were now being bombed. Their supply lines were being cut. And they simply couldn't hold out indefinitely. American factories were running 24 hours a day and were producing more planes, guns and ammunition than the army could even use. Hell, when the Germans wiped out many of the planes in our Squadron in a sneak attack on the base in Alesan, the next morning, the bulldozers just pushed all the plane carcasses aside and new planes arrived that afternoon. We didn't even miss one day of combat – we were just short a few planes for one day. The Germans couldn't stop that and couldn't last indefinitely against it.

If I could stay alive where I was, sooner or later the American army would come to me. The question was whether I could do that for a long enough period of time. I had to do it. There was no choice.

I had to take a leak again. And a crap. Those would be easy now. Spraying worked for the one and burying the other was known even to Boy Scouts. I climbed down from the cave and found a secluded bush to hide behind about 50 feet from the cave. While I was still somewhat nervous and looking over my shoulder, I was comfortable enough that the increased vulnerability associated with taking a dump didn't bother me too much. That was taken care of quickly.

I noticed another one of the water runoff paths. Actually, it was rather interesting. There was a ledge that would have made for a rather picturesque waterfall in the rain. I was just looking at that and contemplating it when a man appeared on the top of it and jumped down onto the path not more than 10 feet from me.

This guy was wearing olive drab pants and a military coat which was hanging open. He was tall, at least six-feet three or four or better, well-built -- and blonde. He looked very German, but curiously he didn't seem to be armed. I didn't like this at all. This guy was big -- bigger than I was and considerably bulkier. This could be trouble.

"Americano?" the guy asked.

I was not going to say anything and gave no response other than a steely-eyed glare.

"Tedeschi?" was the next question.

I did not respond. The guy was smiling and speaking Italian and not German, but we were both clearly more than a little bit tense.

"Catolishi?"

What the hell was that? Catolishi?

"Christe?" he asked.

Still I made no response.

"Christe?" he asked again.

With that, the guy put his feet together, extended his arms out from his sides, laid his head to the side on his shoulder just like Christ when he was crucified on the cross.

"Christe?" he asked again. 'Yes' I nodded. With that, the guy smiled, said "Mi amico!" and came toward me with arms extended like he was going to hug me. What the hell was I to do? Before I could think, I was being hugged and patted on the back by this big bear of a guy who was now my 'amico.' I patted him back. Geez, this was strange!

The guy then stepped back and pointed to himself.

"Renzo," he said. "Io, Renzo."

"Georgio" I responded.

"Ah....Si," Renzo said smiling. Then Renzo started talking. I couldn't make out much, but could make out 'Nello' and 'Beppe.' This guy may have looked German, but he was clearly speaking Italian and he clearly knew something about Nello and Beppe.

We parted amicos. Renzo headed back down the mountain. I wasn't going back to the cave until Renzo was completely out of sight. Once he was, I went back to the cave, went inside and vowed not to ever go out again in the daylight and just shook my head. This was getting a little absurd.

'Sera' is the Italian word for evening. It starts around 4 PM and runs until whenever one goes to bed. 'Notte' is night, but other than saying 'Goodnight' it is rarely used.

Beppe had said 'Sta Sera' which was a colloquial version of 'Questa Sera' -- 'This Evening.'

Around 5 o'clock, Beppe returned to the cave. He had clothes with him -- Italian clothes. I was about to become a real Italian. I was pleased. With Italian civilian clothes, I could pass for Italian. That could explain my lack of understanding of German -- unfortunately, it would not explain my lack of understanding of Italian.

There was some risk to changing into Italian clothes. As long as I was in uniform, I was entitled to be treated as a Prisoner of War if caught. If I were disguised, I would be treated as a spy and probably shot on the spot. Prison Camp would be a whole lot better than death. But I didn't trust the Germans to recognize my POW rights. They could just as easily shoot me on the spot and no one would ever be the wiser. I decided that whether I could pass as an Italian or not, it would be better to be in Italian civilian clothes than an American pilot's uniform. I took off my dog tags and put the civilian clothes on in the cave. I smiled at the result. I almost looked Italian. Beppe smiled too. Later, I buried the dog tags under a thick bush. With them I was clearly a spy. Without them, I had at least a chance of claiming to be an Italian.

Beppe was truly a friend...and a hero. This man was risking his life and probably his family's lives. And he was doing so freely. He was also clearly a thinker. He didn't make wrong moves. And everything he did made sense.

The clothes fit reasonably well. The pants were a little big, but not too much. They seemed to match what I had seen so far in Italy.

Beppe spoke. I didn't understand, but I did catch the name Renzo in there somewhere.

"Renzo?" I asked Beppe.

"Si -- a Renzo," Beppe said pointing toward the clothes. The clothes were Renzo's. So he was a friend and part of this group. That was another big relief -- although the military uniform Renzo had worn still bothered me a bit. And Renzo had scared the shit out of me that morning. I mean REALLY scared me. God, Renzo looked German!

Beppe was taking good care of things. My admiration for this Italian farmer was growing every minute. He sat down and motioned for me to do the same. It was time for my first Italian lesson. We started with some of the basics: the words for I, you, want, eat, food, drink, water, wine, come, go, now, yes, no, and the three hardest words to learn from hand signs: yesterday, today and tomorrow. Those took forever to get across, but I did finally get them.

And it was also time for a shave and I did need one. Beppe had brought a razor and soap along. My beard grew quickly and it was already starting to itch. Beppe motioned that we could go down to the stream, but I wasn't comfortable with that. This would be a dry shave.

I had become accustomed to cold shaves during my time on Corsica, but dry shaves were still dry shaves – slow and painful. I licked my hand and tried to get some lubrication for the soap. It wasn't much. My whiskers pulled. This was not an experience I relished. I left what there was of a mustache as much to minimize discomfort as I did to complete my Italian disguise. The mustache pleased Beppe. I would look more Italian with a mustache than without one.

"Georgio Italiano!" was Beppe's comment when I was done. Yes, I was feeling more and more like an Italian every minute.

Then it was time for more Italian words: please, thank you, thank you very much, here, there, quiet, good, bad, hot, cold, bread, and repetition of the word for Germans – 'Tedeschi.' Beppe also taught me 'Scapare!' which means 'get the hell out of here fast.' That could be crucial and it needed to be learned now. There would be no time to learn it when and if it were needed.

I asked about Nello. I hadn't seen him since the first day and that seemed like an eternity ago. Nello was fine Beppe said. He tried to tell me that he, Beppe, had been put him in charge of caring for me by the Padrone. I didn't know what 'Padrone' meant, but thought that I understood the rest. Nello would be back Beppe said. He just didn't know when.

I asked about the Germans.

"No Tedeschi sta sera," Beppe answered. He tried to explain that most of them had gone elsewhere in a hurry and that the ones who were left in the village would have to stay in their headquarters. I didn't understand any of that, but I did understand 'No Tedeschi sta sera.'

We just sat there in front of the cave for a long time together. We were a lot alike in many ways and felt a real kinship. We liked and trusted each other and were just plain comfortable being together. Things were settled now. I was safe and we both felt good about that.

I asked Beppe about his family.

"'Familia mia?' Beppe asked."

"Si." I replied.

"Mi molgie e Dina." Beppe said.

"Dina," I repeated.

"Mio filio e Gino. Mi filia sono Lina, Graziella, e Bruna."

Beppe had four children: a son, Gino, and daughters Lina, Graziella, and Bruna. I felt very good. I was able to understand at least some basic Italian.

"Anche tu?" Beppe asked.

"Mi moglie e Margi," I replied.

"Filii?" Beppe asked.

"Ora, no," I answered. It was the closest I could get to 'Not yet.' Margie and I had been married for 5 years, but hadn't been able to have children yet -- although not for lack of trying. Given the situation I was in, that was probably fortunate.

"Quanti anni?" Beppe asked.

That took awhile. Those were new words. Ah! How many years? How many years what? Oh...how old! I didn't know any numbers so I used my fingers: 10 + 10 + 6. I was 26.

"Ventisei" Beppe said. That sounded good so I nodded agreement.

"Tu?" I asked?

"Trentanove" Beppe answered and the did the same with his fingers - 39.

We sat some more and then as the sun started to set, it was time for Beppe to go.

"Tedeschi domani?" I asked. I didn't know why Beppe would even know that; it was more just wanting to hear from someone that there wouldn't be any Germans first thing in morning again. Beppe shrugged his shoulders. He didn't know.

"Spero no." he said. 'Spero' -- that was Latin for I hope. I didn't know why I even remembered that -- I hated Latin when I took it in high school, but it was helping. 'I hope not' Beppe had said.

"Anche io" I said with a sigh. 'Me too.' Beppe smiled.

It was not going to be easy living on that mountain -- especially in the nights and the early mornings. But things were good. I would be much safer now.

"Mille grazie, Beppe." I said with a deep sense of gratitude.

"Niente, Georgio. Niente!"

"Buono notte, Georgio." Beppe said as he left.

"Si, buono notte, Beppe. Buono notte e mille grazie!" I said again.

I watched Beppe climb down the mountain. Fate had been very good to me. Very good -- to have such a brave and wonderful man, no three men – Beppe, Nello, and Renzo -- to help me. I wondered whether Dombrowski and Obravatz had had similar luck. The odds against it seemed almost impossible. Then again, the Italians were proving to be a brave and wonderful people. Maybe Dombrowski and Obravatz were OK.

And what about Margie? Would she know somehow that I was safe now and in good care? I knew that she had some strange ESP thing that I never understood and never really quite believed. Maybe it was real. Maybe she would know. I hoped so because she would never imagine what was really happening to me. It was just too unusual to even contemplate from Coatesville, Pa.

But the words. I had to go over the vocabulary words. I had to drill himself on them. I couldn't let them get away from my mind overnight. I started my vocabulary drill mentally saying each Italian word and then it's English equivalent. That would occupy my mind for the evening -- drilling myself on the words and making up sentences, questions and answers.

As the sun set, I slipped into the cave. I put my head down on the half-eaten bread pillow. I continued the language drills until I gradually drifted off to sleep. 'Sta sera' had proven to be 'buona sera.'

Chapter Fourteen
Hunted

The next morning, there were no patrols. The valley, however, was not quiet. I could hear heavy traffic and could only assume that it was German military vehicles moving through the valley to reinforce the front lines to the south. The din was constant from 6 o'clock until 9 and then silence settled in.

About ten o'clock, Beppe, Nello and Renzo all appeared at the entrance to the cave. They all seemed relaxed and happy -- the Germans had moved out -- even if they did figure that it was only temporary. There were no Germans left in the valley except for a couple at the local church and a couple at their headquarters in Barberino di Mugello, the village which was close by.

They had brought food and wine and Renzo even had a camera. I didn't like that, but Renzo was already giving directions for poses in front of the cave. First there were solo shots of each of us. Then there were group shots: Beppe and me, Nello and me, Renzo and me, and then Beppe and Nello and me. On the one hand, I wasn't quite sure of Renzo, who had been in the Italian military and served as a driver for some of the Fascist commanders before the Italian regime fell. On the other hand, Renzo did apparently have some connections and he was OK with Beppe and Nello. The film would have to be hidden until it became safe to have it developed -- when the war was over. But we did take pictures and we, the four comrades, were all smiling and proud. We even went back to the first cave and took one of me there.

We passed much of the day talking -- talking about our families, what things were like in America, and what they were like in Italy. Nello was interested in the ring I wore on a chain around my neck. He was curious about the skull and cross bones on it. That was a symbol sometimes used by

The Family, what Americans know as the Mafia. He wondered if I was an American member.

I laughed when Nello explained that to me. The ring was Margie's graduation ring from nursing school and the symbol was one of several medical symbols frequently used on graduation rings for doctors and nurses. They all laughed when I explained that to them. The Italians were also pleased that I was a family man and devoted to my wife.

They suggested that I come to dinner in the farm house that evening since the Germans were gone. I was uneasy about that but was desperate for some touch of normalcy and a family dinner would certainly be that. I agreed.

Dinner normally started around eight in the summertime. They would place a ladder on the southern side of the house, the one that faced the ravine, the garden and the mountain – and that was farthest away from the church in which the Germans were headquartered. That way I would have complete cover when I came to the house. Beppe would be outside tending the garden and could wave me away if things were not safe.

The late afternoon passed slowly. I was apprehensive about leaving the security of my mountain. But I also wanted to be around normal people in a normal setting again and the strength of that desire made the time pass very slowly. Finally, 7 o'clock came and with the start of the evening shadows, I began making my way down the mountain.

That mountain was beginning to feel like home to me. I headed down the water run-off paths. I was careful, but there had been no signs of Germans all day. I reached the creek and had to make a choice -- I could follow the old dirt road from there or follow the creek. The brush around the creek was very heavy and the creek bed very muddy. It also traversed some steep drops, but it was the safest. I followed the creek down the ravine for the half mile it took to reach the side of Beppe's garden. I slipped a bit, but moved slowly enough not to fall.

I stopped opposite Beppe's garden and listened. There were still no German sounds. What I heard instead were the sounds of children playing in the yard. The lilt of their laughter was as pleasant a sound as I ever expected to hear -- and they were still kids, still playing, here in the middle of an horrendous war.

I heard a woman call them, just like my mother used to summon my brother, Fred, and me when we were young. Despite a few protests over having their playtime ended, they soon went inside and the valley became quiet.

I climbed to the top of the ravine -- just high enough to look over the edge. I could see the garden. I could see Beppe hoeing and weeding and occasionally looking toward the ravine for me. I moved up a little farther and then Beppe spotted me. He signaled that it was OK and as I moved into the garden, Beppe put down his hoe and started to walk around to the front of the house. If anyone were watching, they would concentrate on Beppe's movements.

Just as Beppe disappeared through the front door, I reached the ladder. It led up to a second story window that was open. I looked around several times and then quickly scampered up the ladder.

Beppe was already inside the bedroom and closed the window after I came through. Then we went downstairs to meet the family -- and there were a lot of them to meet! The children were clustered together. They were quiet and a little afraid. They weren't yet sure whether they really wanted to meet an American pilot. They ranged in age from 4 to about 12: there were Beppe's and Dina's children: Graziella, Lina, Bruna, and Gino (the youngest); Renzo and Fernanda's daughter, Franca, a very cute little blondish 8-year old girl, and their son, Piero; and there was Nello's son, Mario.

And then there was Beppe's wife, Dina. She was a tiny woman -- probably just under 5 feet tall; but she was clearly very energetic and very strong. She came over immediately and gave me a big Italian hug. That required a big bend on my part, but with that hug, I also felt human again. There were Beppe's brother, Lindo, and his pregnant wife, Julia -- both of which gave me warm hugs. The process was repeated with Nello's wife, Dina, who was similar in stature to Beppe's wife, Dina. And, it was repeated again in somewhat more reserved fashion with Renzo's wife, Fernanda, who was taller and dressed more formally than the others. There was another woman, Bruna, Beppe's sister. Her hug was the most reserved -- as was fitting for a single woman who had no husband or male companion. She was tall, easily 5'10", statuesque in her bearing and quite beautiful with very deep, sad,

Italian eyes.

I looked around at my new family. There was a moment of silence as they took me in as well. Then Dina Ferri started back to getting dinner ready and what had seemed like a still photograph just seconds before, now appeared to be something akin to Grand Central Station on a holiday -- activity everywhere. The women were all busy and bustling everywhere. The children were starting to push each other closer to the 'Americano' and giggling. And the men all settled into chairs around the kitchen table to have a glass of wine and discuss the events of the day. I always liked kitchen tables -- they were always the focal point of my family's life and this one felt very comfortable -- just like home -- and I had forgotten how good being at home could feel.

I listened closely and was able to discern that there apparently was urgent situation that had caused the Germans to send most of their occupying troops south to Florence. Cassino had been taken and the Americans were moving north. Rome had fallen as well. No one knew what had caused the German troop movements, but they expected at least a few days without any of the Tedeschi disrupting their lives.

The girls pushed Gino, the youngest and only boy in the Ferri family, over to me. He was clearly scared -- at least until Beppe smiled and I picked him up and set him on my knee. I wasn't especially good with kids, but captured Gino's attention and won his favor with the old pull-your-thumb-apart trick. Gino loved it and even the girls came closer to see what this strange Americano named 'Georgio' could do. I was accepted by the kids -- and the grown-ups laughed as well.

The wine was superb! Like most young Americans, I had been known to drink a bit upon occasion. I had always preferred hard liquor; it worked much more efficiently than wine or beer. But this wine was just superb! I learned that it was homemade and wondered if Italian farmers could make wine this good, why the commercial wines I had tasted didn't even come close.

And the food! Sure, it was my first real meal in days, but it was the best I ever remember eating to this day! There was antipasto and then spaghetti like I had never eaten before and, as I was to learn that evening, then came the main course: chicken and vegetables. And during all of that there was wine and more wine. Then there was desert and something called Grappa.

I had never heard of Grappa before, but Beppe insisted that I try it. All the men had a glass and toasted me, themselves, Italy, America, and numerous other things. The wine had already found it's way to my head and the Grappa only accelerated matters. I was relaxed. I was full. And I was feeling no pain -- hardly a condition suited to climbing a mountain in the dark -- but it had to be. One couldn't count on the Germans staying away for even one day. The conversation and merriment continued for a good long while. I switched to cappuccino and tried to sober up a bit. I became very comfortable with all of them as they did with me, but then it was time to go and that fact had a real sobering effect.

I left the same way I had come -- via the ladder. It seemed pointless at night in the pitch darkness of the hillside, but it was the safest. I hugged everyone goodnight and offered many mille grazie's before climbing down. I felt warm, relatively safe, thankful, and happy -- all things I would never have imagined as I descended into this valley by parachute only several days before.

The Germans re-deployed all of their resources with the fall of Cassino and Rome, but their defenses were clearly crumbling in Italy. I was later told that there had been a meeting of the German high command in Italy and that the Americans somehow got wind of it and bombed the meeting place, killing many of their leaders. I have no idea whether this actually happened, but what I do know is that Germans were suddenly on the hunt for each and every downed American they knew about. I think they viewed everyone of us as a possible spy. Beginning the morning after my dinner at the farmhouse, they were after me with a vengeance.

Foolishly, I had spent the night in the first cave since it was the closest to Beppe's farmhouse. I arose with the first light and started lazily and a bit woozily up the mountain to the second cave. I increased my pace when I heard the sounds of German transports back in the valley. I got to my cave and pulled a downed branch in front of the entrance. The war was back. So much for normalcy.

That morning began even more abruptly at Beppe's. Just as everyone started in with their morning's chores, a dozen Germans stormed down the lane. They suspected that Beppe and the others were helping the American who had landed in the valley a few days before. They searched the house hurriedly destroying much as the went through. They gathered all the families together outside for questioning, including the children. They demanded to know where the American pilot was and when no one responded, they lined them all up against the side of the house. Eleven Germans lined up opposite them about 25 feet away. The twelfth, the commander and the only bilingual one among them, stood off to the side. He ordered his troops to raise their weapons and to prepare to shoot. They snapped their rifles into firing position. He told the three families in his cropped Italian that if they didn't tell them where the American pilot was, they would all be shot.

The children did not want to die. They did not want their parents to die. They didn't want their friends to die either.

The parents didn't want to die and they didn't want their children to die. It would have been easy to have told the Germans where the I was. It might have saved their lives, but telling the Germans where I was would also have meant that they had helped me. The Germans would probably, no, they would definitely have shot them for that. If they didn't tell, they might be shot just on suspicion, but then again, maybe they would not. Their chances of survival were best if they said nothing. And it was better that the American remain free to fight the Germans. The Germans were an atrocious and disgusting people in their eyes.

Their hearts were all beating fast and hard. Beppe stepped forward and spoke three words, 'We know nothing.' That was it. Three words. The fate of the three families rested on Beppe and those words. He stepped back and all knew precisely what to do. They were to say nothing. Beppe had just told them his position -- and his position was to be followed. Little Gino grabbed onto Beppe's leg and held on tightly.

Seconds passed. Then more seconds. Then more. The commander was clearly thinking. If they shot the Italians, the gunfire would warn the American or any others in the area and he would take good cover or escape. He could avoid capture for a long time in the mountains. If they didn't shoot the Italians, they might catch the one American that morning, but if not, they could also watch the family closely and hope to ambush him. No, it would suffice to scare the Italians. Shooting them would not accomplish anything.

Finally, the German issued the command -- lower the weapons. He ordered the troops to search the mountain and turned to Beppe. Looking him coldly in the eye, he told Beppe that they would find the cursed American and would kill him, but that until they did, they would be watching Beppe and his family closely. They had better not help him if they wished to live. With that, he turned and joined his troops as they headed up the mountain.

The Germans fanned out and headed up the mountain. There were already patrols covering the adjoining mountain from the bottom to the top. I sat in the mouth of my cave. I thought I heard something, but could see nothing. Then I thought I saw something move way down the mountain. That was enough. There was no margin for error. I crawled to the back of the cave and sat against the back in the most obscured corner. I gathered my burlap sack which was now empty and placed it behind my back as a cushion. I scraped everything I could find in front of me -- leaves, twigs, dirt -- you name it.

I sat and waited and listened. And listened. I could hear footsteps through the brush. The footsteps were getting closer. And closer. My heart was pounding again. I was defenseless. Maybe I should have carried a gun. No. That would only guarantee getting shot. I listened some more. Only footsteps, no talking. This was a serious hunt. I imagined the Krauts using hand signals to communicate as they checked every nook and cranny. Some of the steps were getting closer. I pulled myself in tighter.

I saw the German rifle and bayonet poke the downed branch from the side. It was impossible to see into the cave from below and almost impossible from the sides. They would have to pull the branch off and climb onto the ledge to see me. Another poke. And then the steps moved off. I was safe -- for the moment.

I thought about Beppe. I owed my life to him again. The second cave had made all the difference. It was smaller and much less visible than the first one. They would certainly go into the first cave this time. I wondered if Beppe and Nello and Renzo and their families were all right.

We had been foolish the night before. Had I been seen? If so, Beppe and his family were in great peril. The Germans would not treat them well and might shoot all of them....but there had been no shots. The Germans would have passed the farmhouse on their way up the mountain. I felt a little relieved. At least I thought everyone was safe for the time being.

I sat still and listened some more. I could hear nothing. Every so often I thought I heard movement, but I couldn't be sure. I sat some more and listened. And listened. And listened. I could not afford to move at all. I stayed precisely where I was all day in the same position -- and I was starting to cramp and ache.

Occasionally I could hear the German patrols. They were talking now. Sometimes they sounded close. Sometimes far away. It was clear that they were more relaxed now. They had covered the mountain once and were merely doing repeat checks. I couldn't figure out why I was suddenly so important to them. If I had been spotted the night before, someone would have taken a shot at me then. There would be no reason to wait until morning. No, I couldn't have been spotted then. What the hell had happened? Why were there German patrols all over the mountain and the ones next to it? I couldn't even conjure up a reason.

Evening came and went. I didn't hear any patrols for several hours. I had to relieve myself acutely, but didn't dare until it was dark. I contemplated relieving myself where I was, but didn't know how long I would be holed up there and the odor could get intense. As darkness set in, I very cautiously began moving. I heard no reactions. I stood at the mouth of the cave and strained to look around in the darkness. I could see nothing. The trees provided a very black canopy that masked the stars and their light. I couldn't see anything, but then, in all likelihood, no one could see me either. I squatted and took care of both of bodily functions burying the waste as best I could in the darkness. It had to be buried. There could be no evidence. There was enough dirt and plenty of leaves. I thought I did a good job of it.

I crawled back into the cave. I had debated fleeing at night. I wanted to get away, but had no idea where to go.

"Georgio" I heard whispered outside my cave in the darkness.

"Georgio, e' Nello!"

"Nello!" I whispered back as I moved to the front of the cave and moved the branches away so he could come in. Nello had brought me food, wine and water -- in complete darkness. We whispered back and forth about the events of the day. He told me about the firing squad and the families -- and that no one had talked. It was going to be rough for at least a couple of days and they would only come, if they could at all, at night.

I told him 'No.' I would be fine for awhile with what I now had. They should not risk anything until the Germans calmed down.

"Capish?" I asked him."

"Capish." And with that Nello departed.

I didn't want to put Beppe, Nello, and Renzo and their families at risk any more. A firing squad? Putting children in front of one? These Krauts were as brutal as any race that had ever lived! Master Race? My ass! They were master nothing! They were nothing more than two-bit thugs!

That day made me realize how utterly horrible this war was. The children -- what if the Germans had hurt or killed the children? And over me? I couldn't bear that thought and returned to deciding whether to sleep or to flee right then. There simply was nowhere to flee to. I would stay put and try to sleep. I was tired. I hurt. I needed to eat and drink some water, then sleep. I would need to be at my best tomorrow. With the food and water Nello had brought, I would be. I needed to be. The Germans were certain to return.

Sleep came slowly. Fear and the adrenaline it produces are slow to fade and it is hard to sleep when one is afraid. But sleep did come. And so did morning.

Morning brought German patrols at first light, but they didn't come as close as yesterday. There was nothing to do but sit.

By late afternoon, I was getting extremely thirsty and hungry. I had decided to tightly ration myself on the food and water. I couldn't risk a nap. The Krauts were still patrolling the mountains and I've been known to snore. That was probably OK at night, but it would be stupid during the day. I didn't want to get shot in my sleep. If I were going to die, I wanted to experience every second of life -- even to the end.

I wondered what was going on with Beppe, Nello, Renzo and their families. They wouldn't venture onto the mountain for several more days, but I wanted to know that they were still OK, this morning. But I knew that I wouldn't any time soon.

Afternoon and evening came and went without incident. I relieved myself after dark.

I covered myself with the burlap and drifted off to sleep. I was not especially religious and, quite frankly hadn't even thought of praying, but I had a strange sense that a guardian angel was watching over me. That was an odd thought, but somehow comforting. Maybe I would come out of this OK.

The third day was much the same as the previous two except that I was getting even more cramped and sore. I continued to ration my intake of both food and water, but found thirst incredibly compelling. The water from Nello lasted only a day and a half. It was now gone. I still had most of the food, but I just wanted a glass of water -- not much, just enough to wet my whistle. I laughed to myself -- a glass of water! Where the hell would I ever get a glass? To hell with that, I just wanted water and I would drink it out of anything. Water. I wanted water.

As the evening shadows came, I knew that I had no choice. I had to get some water and it had to be that evening. I was getting weak and I would not make it for another day. I thought of the stream, I had to go there first, but I decided to try for the farm as well. There hadn't been any German patrols since about two o'clock. Maybe the manhunt was over.

I snuck down the water run-off paths as the light faded. I stopped at the stream, cupped my hands and drank. The cool mountain water tasted tremendous. I drank until I thought I had enough. I filled the empty water bottle from Nello. But I also wanted some additional food. I had no idea how long I was going to be pinned down. More water would have been a good idea as well, but I had left the other bottle, the one filled with wine, at the cave.

I hid the bottle of water and then followed the stream down into the ravine by Beppe's garden. I stopped and thought. Beppe might still be gardening, but wouldn't be expecting me -- not with all the Germans still around. I hoped that Beppe would be checking the edge of the ravine for me.

As darkness set in, I crawled up to the top of the ravine and could see Beppe in the garden. He was gardening after dark -- maybe he was waiting for me. I waited to see if he were looking toward the ravine for me, but he wasn't, at least not that I could tell. I looked all around and couldn't see any Germans. It was now or never.

I snuck into the garden. I weaved between plants and bushes and came up behind Beppe. I couldn't afford a sound and decided to grab Beppe and cup my hand over his mouth. I did that in a flash. I felt Beppe tense with fear and then relax when I said, "Beppe, e' Georgio." I released my grip and Beppe turned toward me.

"Mangiare, Beppe! Mangiare per favore!" I whispered with as much urgency as I could put into a whisper. I needed more food!

"Si. Si!" he answered.

Beppe went into the house and then came out with some loaves of bread and a salami - and two bottles of wine. He brought them to me at the edge of the ravine.

"Beppe, no vino! Aqua per favore." I whispered. Wine was great, but I needed more water in my cave, not wine.

It took me awhile to translate Beppe's response 'Water is to wash with. Wine is to drink.' I was going to be on my own for water. But I now had enough food for a real siege.

At the time, Beppe's giving me wine instead of more water aggravated me, but as time passed, I came to appreciate both the gesture and his response -- water *is* to wash with, wine's to drink – at least in Italy. The phrase perfectly symbolized Italy and the Italian outlook on life. The finer things are to be tasted, savored, and enjoyed - at all times and especially in the worst of times. They are the essence of life - what makes it worth living. The mundane? The mundane things are simply to be used, endured, or ignored. There was a major lesson in Beppe's response for me, even if it did take me awhile to appreciate it.

Beppe indicated that Tedeschi were everywhere and looking for me. There was no time for a water vs. wine discussion and I knew it.

"Scapare!" Beppe whispered as he motioned toward the mountain.

"Mille grazie, Beppe! Io scapare!" I answered and immediately turned and headed back up the ravine for the mountain.

I couldn't handle going back up through the ravine. I was weaker than I thought. I just couldn't make it. I had probably consumed enough water between Nello's bottle and my stop at the stream, but I had rationed myself too tightly on the food. Now my legs were weak, just when I needed them. I climbed out of the ravine and into the brush between it and the dirt road. I ate some bread and salami. I was still very thirsty, but I hadn't gotten back to my hidden bottle of water, so I drank some wine. The wine seemed to quench my thirst. I just sat there repeating that process until half a loaf of bread, half the salami and one of the bottles of wine were gone.

I tried to get up and couldn't. The wine had gone straight to my head and I was quite dizzy, quite weak, and quite exhausted. I collapsed in the brush and slept.

I awoke just before morning and was completely and totally desperate for water. I grabbed the bottles, the bread and the salami and headed back toward the stream. I slid down the ravine, set the bread, wine bottles and salami on the side and dove in. I buried my face in the three inches of water and drank and drank and drank. I have never felt such an obsession in my life. I *had* to have water. And this cool mountain water was good!

Finally, after drinking until my belly was about half full, I raised my head and looked upstream. About 50 feet upstream was one of Beppe's cows. It was not just standing there or drinking, it was relieving itself right into the water! I just laughed -- even cold mountain cow piss tasted great! And it wouldn't hit me like the wine had done the night before. I laughed again and stuck my head back in the stream for a few more gulps. Cow piss or no cow piss, I had to have water! Finally, I felt the compulsion subside and I grabbed my food and wine and went upstream past the cow and drank some more. I drank until I felt I could drink no more.

My head was hurting from last night's wine and the coldness of the water. My belly was full and I felt more alive and able to cope than I had for the last two days. I would survive.

I found a small pool and filled the empty wine bottle with water and decided to head back to my cave before the morning light became bright, picking up my hidden bottle of water along the way.

I slogged back up the mountain to my cave. I was dripping water everywhere, but didn't care. I did make sure to venture off the run-off paths occasionally. I checked behind for Germans frequently, but there were no signs of any -- yet. I doubted that they would track me by my drippings.

I settled into the cave again being careful to pull the downed branch in front just like it had been. I put my hands on my stomach. It was full and that felt good -- both inside and out.

I broke off some bread. This was almost like Communion -- wine and bread. I bit off some salami. Maybe I could convince the churches to add salami to Communion. This was great! Anyway, my Communions thereafter would always involve wine, bread, *and* salami. I was very thankful -- thankful for the sustenance, the stream, the cave, and for Beppe, Nello, and Renzo, my protectors. How could all of this be explained? It couldn't. Despite the events of the last three days, at that point and for no apparent reason, I truly felt that I was going to be safe.

The rest of that morning passed quietly. There were patrols, but they were off in the distance. I spent the time wedged into the back of the cave. My head was throbbing from the wine, but my belly was very full. I would have gladly traded the bread and salami for a couple of aspirin, but by noon my head had stopped throbbing. I was glad I hadn't had the chance to trade them away.

Chapter Fifteen
Garden Gourmet On The Run

I thought more and more about my Italian friends and their children. I couldn't bear the thought of the children being involved. I had to get out of there. As long as I was there, the children were at risk.

I decided to wait one more day before setting out. The bread and salami would help me with my strength and I could get some more food from Beppe's garden that night. By the next morning, I would be back to normal.

I stayed in the cave all day. There were no sounds of German patrols during the afternoon and I moved around a bit. Periodically, I ate some bread and salami and sipped some water. I quietly exercised my legs and arms. They seemed to be getting a whole lot stronger than they had been the evening before.

When night came, I left the cave and headed down for Beppe's garden. I wanted more food. I needed more food - something fresh and juicy. I stopped for some more water at the stream. I drank some and filled one empty wine/water bottle. I moved slowly down the ravine taking one step at a time. It was very dark and I could barely see anything. I didn't want to misstep and create a lot of noise. I climbed to the top of the ravine and could see Beppe's house on the plateau in the moonlight. It was a beautiful sight, but this was not a sightseeing trip.

I went back into the ravine and continued until I was opposite Beppe's garden. I climbed from the ravine and snuck into the garden just as I had done the evening before. This time, however, I had a problem. There was no Beppe and I knew nothing about gardening. Despite the moonlight, I could not identify any of the plants except the tomato plants and I knew that the tomatoes on the vine were not ripe.

I had to eat, but what? Well, here's how you eat at night in an Italian garden

-- you pull up a plant, scrape off the dirt, then take a bite off the top and chew it, then spit it out. Then you take a bite from the bottom, chew it, and spit it out. Whichever tastes better, that's what you eat.

The bottom of the first plant tasted much better than the top, so I ate the bottom. I waited a few minutes to see what would happen. Nothing did. My stomach was fine with it. I felt very primitive having to explore what plants or parts of plants were edible and which were not. My respect for early man increased immensely. I was very grateful that I had the advantage of knowing that at least some part of every plant was edible -- this was Beppe's garden. I pulled up and ate several adjacent plants. They tasted the same and were fine.

The bottom of the next plant was also the more tasty. So I ate several of those. On the third, the top tasted better, not good, just better, so I ate the top. I could recognize none of the tastes, but so far everything was sitting well enough in my stomach. Then came the onion. That taste I knew -- and didn't like. I spit it out quickly. I may have been in a desperate situation, but I still wasn't desperate enough to eat an onion, not when the other plants tasted decent enough.

"Margie loves onions," I thought. She would have feasted on them until morning. Not me! I hated them -- hated the taste, hated the texture, hated the smell.

I had always disdained vegetables and was now feasting on them. For all I knew, I was eating raw broccoli, asparagus, cauliflower, spinach, and Brussels sprouts. Margie would be pleased with that, but would then want to deliver a five-minute speech on their merits and would probably try to force me to eat them with every meal for the rest of my life. If I ever got back to her, it would be a long time before I would tell her about this vegetable feast in the garden. This was here -- it was war and survival. That was there -- one only had to eat what one liked.

I laughed silently to myself and then returned to whatever it was that I was eating. I hoped that it wasn't goddamned Brussels sprouts because whatever it was, it surely tasted good.

I finished eating. I had no sense of time at night and couldn't see my watch well enough. I tried to follow the moon and note it's position, but that was hard on the mountain because of the tree cover. I knew that there still had to be quite a few hours until daylight. I felt good enough and strong enough to travel. I decided to head west toward the coast.

I climbed back up the mountain and passed my cave. I picked up my sack and just kept going up. My cave was about a five hundred feet below the peak. Once I reached the peak, I stood there for awhile trying to get a fix on some landmark on the other side. That was hard. The only thing I could make out was another peak across another valley. I could see nothing below, only an occasional set of headlights along a road far below.

I decided to go half way down the mountain and wait for first light. If my position appeared to be safe, I would remain there until nightfall and observe and then move on. If not, I would find some place to hide and go somewhere else.

I slowly made my way down the western side of the mountain. When I figured that I had reached the halfway point, I stopped. Actually, I slipped off a small cliff that I couldn't see in the dark. It was about ten feet high and I hit the ground hard and fell. My feet and ankles hurt and that fall had convinced me that I should not go any farther. The next cliff might just be high enough to kill me.

I found a full bush and curled up under it and dozed until dawn.

Once morning came, I could see that the valley below was much narrower than the valley on my side of the mountain. My side? I was already feeling at home there. I was learning it well. It was mine. On this side there was no Beppe, Nello, or Renzo. I was on my own.

I could see the road. It was a narrow and twisting road running north and south with the valley. I could also see what I thought was a railroad track. That made sense. That would be the line that we had bombed when we were shot down. I could see some houses spaced irregularly along the road.

Then I saw the Germans. They were everywhere. There were personnel carriers, a few tanks parked under some trees for cover, and some odd looking vehicles that I could only imagine were the German equivalent of Jeeps. Nothing was moving. They were just all parked along the road.

Getting through that valley would be tough. I would be OK if I got through and reached the mountain on the other side. But nothing was moving. I watched some more. They were clearly occupying the area and that meant a lot of Germans and patrols. I decided to simply watch and stay put for the day. That would also give my feet and ankles a day to recover.

I heard no sounds of patrols on the mountain. I felt reasonably safe crawling out from under the bush occasionally to see what was doing. Not much was. Everything seemed to be quiet. That was good. We must have hit the railroad bridge or there would have been trains. We must have also gotten the road or there would be north-south traffic -- reinforcements going south. I was proud of that. We had cut a supply line. To be sure, it would be rebuilt and others used in the meantime, but every success for us was a defeat for Gerry -- and would make taking Italy all the easier for the ground troops.

I watched some more. There were too many Germans for me to have a realistic chance of getting through. They were protecting their supply line and would do so intensely until it was rebuilt. Heading west was not going to be an option. I decided to return to my cave on the other side of the mountain. I could eat from Beppe's and other gardens at night and sustain myself for a long time.

I stayed under the bush for most of the evening. I wanted to watch the Germans to see if anything was moving at night. It wasn't. Then, as the shadows grew long and the sun sank behind the peak of the mountain on the other side of the valley, I started my climb back over the peak to my side of the mountain.

I was getting good at moving at night, my one fall notwithstanding. The runoff paths made things pretty easy. They were a bit hard to see, but one almost developed a sense for them. I felt a great sense of relief when I reached the peak and started down my side of the mountain. Finding my cave would be tough coming down from above instead of up from below, but I did have a good idea where it was.

I moved very cautiously. I still didn't want to make any loud sounds, but I was far up and away from any possible Germans. It seemed like an eternity going down the mountain -- much like getting to one's destination on vacation. That was a strange thought -- a vacation in the middle of a war. I could certainly use a vacation -- just one day's fishing at Black Lake in New York. That would certainly be lovely right now. Those were stupid thoughts, but I indulged them anyway. They were good thoughts and provided some relief. But I had to find my cave, not dream about the joys of fishing -- at least not all night.

Finally, I recognized my location. I was on a familiar path below my cave. Just knowing where I was was a great relief. I would be home in 5 minutes. I turned and headed up and approached 'home' cautiously. I looked and listened. There were no sounds. It was safe. I climbed onto the ledge, moved the branch and replaced it, then crawled into my niche in the back and fell sound asleep -- just like a baby being placed in its crib after a long journey.

Morning brought a gentle rain outside the cave. There was a stillness with it -- a gentle sound. There would not likely be any patrols in the rain, but the gentle sound of the rain would mask the sounds if there were. It would not be a good day to do anything but stay put. I was grateful for the cave. It kept me dry. I decided to sleep some more.

The rain stopped around noon and the sun came out shortly thereafter. The smells were incredible. Everything smelled fresh and wonderful. I was sure that it smelled just as wonderful after a rain at home, but I had never noticed it. Here with all of my senses on alert all the time, everything was much more intense -- including the smells.

I crawled to the front of the cave and looked around the mountain. It was beautiful. I could see the bell tower of the church which was about a half mile from Beppe's. It looked like a lovely, small Italian church. I thought that I would like to go inside sometime, but that's where the Germans had their field headquarters. Any visit would have to wait until they moved out.

I sat at the entrance to my cave for a long time and simply took everything in. This was an incredibly beautiful country! My thoughts returned to Beppe and Dina and the other families. I kept thinking about the children. I did not want the children placed at risk on my account. I had to move. West was out. I would try South next.

I napped some in the afternoon and awoke just as evening was beginning. There had been no patrols at all so I felt safe getting started before darkness.

Monte Maggiore was the larger mountain just to the south of my mountain. It was a huge obstacle, but it would be safe. It took most of the late afternoon and early evening to get to it and up one side. When I looked down from near the summit, I saw yet another valley to the South. This one was much wider than the one to the West. The Americans were to the South, several hundred miles to the south, but at least there was the prospect of getting back to them.

I moved around Monte Maggiore to the West. I could see the narrow valley again. It opened into a wider plain and a small city. I wished that I knew the name of it -- or had a map. It looked rather industrial. I tried to remember the names of the other targets in that area. I couldn't. Bombardiers learned the areas and landmarks. Pilots just flew the planes.

There was no hope of moving through a small city undetected. I would try to go through the wider valley to the south. I went back around the peak of Monte Maggiore. At nightfall, I would start down.

I moved cautiously but quickly down the mountain that night. Once I got to the base of Monte Maggiore, I was able to cover distances much more quickly. As daylight began to break, I reached the ridge on the other side of the valley. I climbed desperately to get close to the top of it. By my guess, I had covered at least 4 or 5 miles.

I looked everywhere for hiding places and could find nothing suitable. Oh, there were plenty of dense bushes, but no caves. No real security. I did not like feeling insecure. I sat down and rested next to a bush. As always, I watched and listened. There were no German patrols on this ridge. There were Germans all over the valley, but they had either stopped their fervent man-hunting patrols or had figured that no Americans were in this area.

I napped part of the afternoon under the bush trying to keep one eye and both ears open. That was more concept than reality, however. I had been up almost 24 hours and I needed sleep. And when I slept, I slept.

At night, I climbed over the top of the ridge and started surveying the countryside on the other side. There was a lot of what could only be German activity. There were headlights everywhere and everything seemed to be moving. This area was far more intensely occupied than anywhere I had been. Perhaps I was getting close to the outskirts of Florence. I didn't know. What I did know was that going farther South was not going to be good or easy.

I sat and thought for awhile. Could I do several hundred miles like this without getting caught or killed? The prospects seemed slim. I wanted desperately to get back to American troops, but there were just too many Germans and other obstacles between here and there. There was only one realistic alternative -- return to my mountain and live from the gardens at night until the Americans came to me. But I would not make contact with my Italian friends and put them in peril again.

I didn't want to spend another day protected only by a bush so I headed north back toward my mountain and cave that night. I crossed the wide valley nervously but easily and was soon moving up the southern side of Monte Maggiore. I was tired, but kept going and climbed up near the peak. I found a good bush and slept.

I spent the day on Monte Maggiore. It was July 3rd by my calculation. I had been there for almost two weeks and was still alive and free. That was miraculous! I had spotted some orchards and gardens when I was returning the night before. I decided to eat from them that evening. They were far away from any houses and appeared to be quite safe.

As the sun set, I moved down the mountain. I was feeling weak again and desperate for water -- having emptied my last water bottle. I tried the orchard first. There were some pear trees. I feasted on them. They seemed to quench both my hunger and thirst. I decided not to risk going into the gardens and I had not passed any streams nearby. I climbed back up Monte Maggiore, found a suitable bush and went to sleep.

It was very cool that night up on Monte Maggiore. I shivered often. I awoke with the first light and started rubbing myself for warmth. I found a sunny spot and first stood facing the sun and then turned around warming my back. That warmed me up fast.

It was now the 4th of July -- Independence Day. I would have given anything to see an American flag, hear the Star Spangled Banner, watch a parade or a fireworks display. I climbed higher up on Monte Maggiore to see if I could get a better view.

The tree cover got thinner. I found a clearing. I didn't go into it, but found a spot on the upper edge where I could see both of the valleys I had visited. I sat there for most of the day trying to piece together what the Germans were doing.

Around 6:30 PM, I got my 4th Of July wish -- the fireworks started. I heard the familiar and wonderful sound of American bombers in the distance. It was a low roar, but one I knew very well. I looked in the sky to the Southwest. I saw the first box of B-25's. Then the second. Then there were what seemed to be wave after wave of B-25's bombing the German positions in both valleys. Judging from the explosions, they were hitting munitions and fuel supply dumps -- and with considerable precision. I remembered that there were rail yards in Prato and Florence. And where there were rail yards, there were fuel and munitions dumps. I guessed that Prato was in the valley to the Southwest and that the outskirts of Florence were to the South.

The B-25's had to be from Corsica! There simply weren't any other B-25 Bomb Groups within range. I felt great -- I was going to get to watch my Group at work.

The display was as dramatic as any 4th of July fireworks display I had ever seen. I felt what I could only imagine as the same pride that Francis Scott Key felt when he watched the bombs bursting over Fort McHenry in Baltimore Harbor. My chest filled with pride and I wondered if my old crew, Holley, Semenak, Dick, Coombs and Cordell were part of the mission. I hoped that they were and that I would someday be able to tell them about watching them from my perch on top of the mountain.

In 20 minutes, the bomb run was over and I headed back toward my mountain. By the next morning's first light, I was at home on my mountain and in my cave. I had been gone for three days and felt as glad to be home as I'd ever felt.

Chapter Sixteen
Dina!

The German patrols were late my first morning at home. They didn't come onto the mountain until about 10 am. They didn't come as high -- didn't even get close to the cave. They talked openly as they searched. Clearly, they were just making routine patrols. They must have figured that I had fled. They had figured right -- but not right enough. I had returned!

"No margin for error" I reminded myself. "No margin for error." I sat in the back of the cave all day, but somehow that day was different. My thoughts were different. I thought of Margie. Did she know I was alive? Did she know what I was going through? Could she know? I missed her terribly. I wanted to see her again, to hold her and kiss her. Would I? I didn't want to think about that. I was not going to be able to get back on my own. I would have to survive until the American troops got to me. But what if they didn't? What if? Could there really be a question of it? No. The tide of the war had turned. The Allies had invaded both Italy and France. It would take awhile, but they would defeat Germany. It was just a question of when -- and it could be a long time. There was no 'what if they didn't.'

I thought about Coatesville. It was hilly there too. The hills weren't as big as these, but some were steep. I was used to hills. Thank God I wasn't from Kansas or some other flat place in the Midwest. I was at home on hills. In fact, when I had been in training in the south, I had taken several flights in the AT-6 trainer, flights just to build flying time, to areas where there were hills. I had just needed to see hills -- like at home.

I thought about the rest of the family: my brothers Fred in Wilmington, French in Coatesville, and Walt out on the farm in Doe Run.

I thought a lot about my sister, Beck, who was an Army nurse. Beck had been the first in the family to enlist. She had done one tour in the far east. I wondered where she was now and how she was doing. The last I knew, she had been re-assigned to another tour of duty -- in India, Burma or somewhere thereabouts. I never did understand how she could deal with all the blood and guts that went with nursing -- especially combat nursing. But I was glad that there were people like her.

I thought about my mother -- Elsie. I missed her. She died just before Pearl Harbor in 1941. I cried like a baby when she died. It was the only time I could ever remember crying in my life. Here I was, just three years later behind enemy lines in a war she didn't even know we were in. She wouldn't have been in favor of my enlisting at first, but she would have been proud of it. And of the pilot's wings. I knew that.

"Georgio! Georgio!" I heard someone call. But who was it? It was a woman's voice.

"Georgio! Georgio!"

I crawled to the front of the cave.

Again, "Georgio. Georgio!" It was Beppe's wife, Dina. What was she doing up here? This was no place for a woman!

"Ciao, Dina!" I answered as I crawled out of the cave. It was late afternoon.

"Ciao, Georgio!"

Dina had brought me some more bread and salami, and some fruit -- apples and pears and did they ever look good -- and some cheese and a wine bottle full of water. This was one thoughtful and very strong and courageous woman!

"Grazie, Dina! Mille grazie!" I said.

I had not eaten since the pear feast in the orchard two nights before. I needed more food and this would be a veritable feast.

I asked about Beppe and the family. Dina answered. She was a bit harder to understand than Beppe. She talked faster and it was harder for me to pick out key words. I did understand that they were all OK, but something was not 'sicuro.' What was that? 'Sicuro?' 'Secure?' Yes, that made sense...it was not secure....not safe. I certainly understood that.

"Si, Dina. No e sicuro. No sicuro per tu, per Beppe, per sua famiglia. Io sono sicuro a qui. Scapare, Dina. Scapare....e mille grazie!"

Dina smiled. She understood just fine -- and I understood the situation. She smiled and gave me a hug -- a strong, Italian hug. That made me feel very good. My mother, Elsie, had been tall -- almost 5'10". Dina was short, but her hug made me feel just right -- just like my mother's and Beck's had always done. I smiled as I watched her scamper down the mountain. She was agile, strong, and courageous. Very courageous! She was a person to be admired and respected -- very much like Beppe.

I still couldn't understand the courage of these people and their devotion to me. But I surely was thankful that I had found them....or rather that they had found me. So much for not re-establishing contact with them.

The evening was settling in fast. I watched and listened for any signs of movement -- any German patrols. There were no sounds other than the birds chirping in the trees. Birds chirping. They had annoyed me before. I had been focused on listening for human sounds and the bird sounds had blocked them out and had scared me. Now, I could just hear the birds chirping. What a lovely sound.

I sat in the mouth of the cave and started with an apple. It was firm and juicy. The taste was sweet, so sweet! I had some cheese as well. I had noticed that after the dinner the other evening, everyone sliced their fruit and cheese and ate them together. I had never thought of combining the two, but this was very, very good. Exquisite actually. And the pears were even better...and juicier and sweeter. This was a feast even if I was eating desert first!

I ate some bread and salami taking bites of each and chewing them together to approximate a sandwich. But I didn't want to eat too much. I had to save some until tomorrow. It was still not safe. I took an inventory: one bottle of wine left over from Beppe's 'Water's-to-wash-with-wine's-to-drink' speech; one bottle of water, half a loaf of bread, half a salami, a wedge of cheese, and several apples and pears. That was a lot. Hell, I might even have breakfast tomorrow!

I put everything into my burlap sack and just sat for awhile. I felt stronger. A lot stronger. I was amazed at how debilitated one could become in just a few days. I would not let that happen again. I would have to feed myself regularly - even if it was only at night from Beppe's garden. But for the time being, I was just fine. Quite fine!

That evening was beautiful. The sun was bright, the sky blue. The Tuscan hills and mountains were a deep green. The rooftops of the Italian houses were all terra cotta. The walls were all cream colored. The valley was all different shades of lighter greens. This was one incredibly beautiful country. And I had a safe and lovely perch from which to take it all in up on the mountain. And that day, I actually had dinner -- salami, bread, water, wine, fruit, and cheese -- all of which was brought to me by a wonderful and courageous friend. War or no war, in some ways life just couldn't get any better.

My life, it seemed, had been filled with strong and courageous women. First, there was Elsie, who raised and supported all four of us kids after Dad died. Then there was Beck, who contributed to those efforts while growing up and even more so once she had become a nurse. And then she went off to war. Then there was Margie, who had supported my becoming a pilot. She too was nurse and good at dealing with life's tougher side. And now there was Dina, who brought food to me on the mountain in the middle of the war. Yes, some very courageous women!

Men and women were certainly quite different -- but not when it came to strength and courage. We just operated in different arenas. It felt very good to have Dina watching over me just as Elsie, Beck, and Margie had done. Dina made it feel like home. 'Thank God for the food and water,' I thought. 'No, thank Dina...amazing Dina!'

As the sun set behind the mountain, I ventured out away from the cave just to look around some more. I was in a *very* beautiful place – and it was, in every respect, now my home.

As the next morning's light crept over the valley, I felt a peacefulness come over me. There was nowhere to go. I had ruled out all possible directions. I had at least a day's food in the sack. While I had resigned to breaking off contact with my Italian friends for their safety, they were still there and still helping me. There was tremendous comfort in that.

It was clear that I was going to be there for a good long time and my mountain was as good a place to be as one could find in the middle of a war – and I was with as good a group of people as there were anywhere.

Chapter Seventeen
The Good Life

The Germans had apparently written me off and seemed very busy with other things. Regular patrols ceased. I had visits from Beppe, Nello, and Renzo. I expressed my concerns with regard to the children and, while my concerns were appreciated, Beppe, Nello, and Renzo all assured me that they and their children were already in the war regardless of whether I was there or not. The children would be fine as long as war, rather than harassing the locals, continued to require most of the attention of the occupying Germans. And from what they had heard, the Allies were defeating the Germans on all fronts.

I was again invited to dinner at the farmhouse and accepted. The dinner came and went without incident. The food was absolutely incredible -- chicken soup with tiny round balls of pasta, fried chicken, some vegetables that tasted very similar to whatever it was I had eaten in the garden at night (and I did not want to know what they were called), a sweet desert, some fruit and cheese, and, or course, some wine and some Grappa. This time, I gave the Grappa the respect it deserved.

I met Beppe's brother, Lindo, and his wife, Julia, again. Julia was clearly very pregnant with their first child. She was due any day. The prospect of bringing new life into a world immersed in war seemed incongruous at first, but the fact of the matter is that life continues and renews itself, even in the middle of wars. Lindo and Julia were clearly very much in love and they were doing what most such people do - starting a family - war or no war.

Then there was a second dinner. And a third. And a fourth. And then there were guests. Italian social life largely revolves around big dinners -- many family members, but also many friends. I was nervous about the guests at first and even more nervous about Renzo's taking pictures of me with each man who visited. Yet they all seemed to want to be part of helping the American.

Renzo explained that the pictures were good because there could be a lot of talk in the village about Georgio, but if there were a picture of everyone with me, all would have good reason to be cautious about what they said and to whom. Not only would the pictures make good mementos and proof of their assisting an American, they would help keep things safe for me. I had progressed from being Beppe's, Nello's, and Renzo's mission – I was now the village's mission!

And so my life progressed -- sleeping in the cave at night, surveying the countryside from my perch during the daytime, and being the center of the village's attention every evening. No one would ever believe it. Hell, even I didn't believe it!

One dinner was particularly enjoyable. A young boy, maybe 14 or 15 years old, from the village of Barberino di Mugello, joined the families for dinner. He seemed quite serious and reserved. In my best broken Italian, I asked him why he was there. He replied that he had met a great American and wondered if I knew him. He then pulled out a piece of paper and proudly showed me the autograph of Edward P. Dombrowski, Heavyweight Champion of the United States.

Ed had, in fact, been a Middleweight Golden Gloves Champion in Pennsylvania at 19 and had been a boxer in the Army and won some sort of regional title. But Heavyweight Champion of the United States? That was Ed -- never content to leave a good story un-enhanced. And, believe it or not, that type of enhancement is just what might keep you alive when you find yourself with people of unknown allegiance. This guy was, indeed, a survivor. I really liked that guy!

Although I was quite taken aback by Ed's rapid rise to boxing fame, I was never inclined to ruin a good story with facts -- even if it weren't my own story.

"Yes, I know Ed," I responded quickly. And not only did I know him, I was on the same crew with Dombrowski when we were shot down. I recounted Ed's feats in getting the escape hatch open in the middle of the fire. I emphasized Ed's courage and strength.

I told the young boy that Ed had won the boxing title by knocking out Joe Louis in the second round of their heavyweight fight in January of 1943. I further told him that Ed was such a great fighter that the ringside experts were unanimous in stating that Ed could have put Joe Louis away in the first round, but out of respect for the great but aging champion, Ed delayed the knockout until the second round. I told them that after this victory, he immediately renounced his title and declared that he would not fight again until his country had won the war against the Nazi oppressors. The boy thought this was a noble gesture and I felt quite proud of elevating Ed from U. S. Champion to a great patriotic athlete who put pride and patriotism above monetary rewards.

The boy then told me that Dombrowski had been helped by the Partisans and that he had probably already returned to the American troops, maybe even to Corsica. That made me feel very good. Ed had saved my life and it was gratifying to know that someone actually made it back to safety. I was curious about the Partisans and whether they could help do the same for me, but I didn't raise the issue. I would trust Beppe, Nello, and Renzo. They were the reason I was alive and they would know whether to ask those questions.

Beppe and Renzo had, in fact, made some inquiries, but they were not confident about the Partisans. And there could be no assurance that the Partisans could get me back to Corsica even if they were willing to try. I was safer where I was. And there I stayed.

The months of August and September were easy. There was a lot of German activity, but it was all in retreat. The Americans were clearly advancing and pushing them back up the Italian boot toward the Alps. The traffic through the valley was constant, day and night -- but most of it was now northbound. The Germans were clearly on the run and concentrating on fortifying Futa Pass a few miles to the north of Barberino di Mugello. There they would make a fierce stand hoping to use the narrow confines of the mountain pass to keep the Allies from advancing farther.

With all of the Germans' attention devoted to the retreat and the fortification of the pass, my life had become predictable and quite safe.

My mornings were leisurely -- watching, smelling, feeling, and thinking more and more about home. My afternoons? Hell, many afternoons were spent in front of my cave visiting with Beppe, Nello, Renzo, and men from the village -- sometimes as many as a dozen at a time – and they would bring bread, wine, cheese, and salami. The wine would flow. Everyone would be talking at once and by that time, I had picked up enough of the language to join in on these warm-hearted gatherings. We did what men do -- talked about politics, the War, wives, families, fishing, hunting, and other sports -- just having a good time.

What I learned from those discussions was that people are very much the same everywhere. Cultures may be different in emphasis, but the basics of being human are quite universal. We're all very much the same - with the same joys and the same problems.

I will also admit that sometimes during those gatherings I felt a few pangs of guilt. There I was, a celebrity at a mid-afternoon wine party, getting half crocked while my wife was back in the States with a piece of paper stating that I was "missing in action." But such is war.

It was also during this time that I really came to know my protectors very well. Our previous interactions had been limited in scope and duration to my survival -- not a lot of time for long discussions. The dinners, were, of course, different, but the days August and September were about getting to know each other much, much better.

As different as they were in temperament – Beppe, the calm, rational, and thoughtful one with a wry sense of humor; Nello - the exuberant, emotional, conversant and active one; and Renzo - the charming, outgoing, and worldly one -- were very much alike in many ways: courageous, passionate, dedicated, and intensely loyal to family and friends. My estimation and enjoyment of each of them increased tremendously during this period -- and they were already rather high.

I've always tried to accept people as they are, but long ago learned to judge people when the chips are down. These men had all come through for me when my chips were as down as they could be. These were my friends -- for life. And they were wonderful, interesting, and charming people. And Beppe! I have never met a man as great as Beppe.

What I also learned from these men -- and from their wives as well -- was that helping each other -- and on a one-to-one basis -- is perhaps the best thing we humans can do for each other. While I doubted that I would ever have the opportunity to help a downed pilot, I did resolve to help people thereafter to the extent that I was able to do so -- and to never ask for anything in return -- just as my Italian friends had done for me.

And the other men from the village, well, they were interesting and enjoyable too. I remember Emilio and Danilo, but there were just so many -- far too many for me to remember them all. But they were and are still my friends.

My evenings during that period were spent more and more having dinner at Beppe's. I was very much a part of the family.

Yes, it was a good life -- a very good life, even in the middle of a war!

Chapter Eighteen
Ed's Journey South

Ed didn't have it nearly as good as I did. He was burned up pretty badly and had taken several hits from our ammunition. He was captured by the Germans almost as soon as he landed – and he landed in the same valley that we had just bombed. Luckily, he was not shot and an Italian doctor was brought to see him for treatment of his wounds.

When he and the doctor were alone, the doctor told him of treating another American, a Tenente Georgio who had been brought to him by some other German sentries. The description seemed to fit me pretty well – although it also fit Obravatz pretty well too – and that's who it really was. But Ed thought I was alive – at least for awhile. The doctor also told Ed that if he could connect with the Partisans, they would help him.

But the Germans weren't about to let him walk away. Once his burns and wounds were dressed, he was sent to join a group of prisoners who were being sent to POW camps in Germany.

They weren't being sent by truck or rail. We had just blown up the bridge on the only railroad heading north and we had apparently gotten the road pretty well too. They were walking the prisoners north - at least as far as Bologna where they would be put onto cattle cars and shipped to the POW camps.

They hadn't gone more than a few miles and – now keep in mind that Ed has some pretty severe burns and several bullet holes in him – when some Allied fighters came over and started to strafe what they perceived to be a German troop column headed north. They couldn't have known that 'troops' were largely made up of POW's, they just saw a troop column in German-held territory and started strafing them.

As soon as the strafing began, everybody headed for cover and ran into the woods. Most found safety behind the trees and rocks, but Ed just kept going. Luckily for him, the German guards were also taking cover and never saw him leave. By the time they discovered that he was missing, it was way too late.

Ed hooked up with the Italian Partisans. They got him civilian clothes and cared for him until his wounds started to heal.

While they were helping him, Ed didn't completely trust the Partisans. He told them whatever he thought would best assure his survival. The defeating-Joe-Louis story was an insurance policy. He even signed autographs - not for his ego, but so that when the Americans finally took the area, they would be able to track him by his autographs – if he did not make it back on his own.

Ed also promised the Italians who helped him all sorts of economic aid after the war - tractors and other farm implements, cars, trucks – whatever he sensed those whom he encountered needed. Hell, so did just about every American who found himself behind the lines. In fact, that was one of Ed's beefs. The further south he got, the more downed Americans had already been through any given area and the more that had already been promised – he had to keep upping the ante!

But as fate would have it, the Marshall Plan, which the Allies implemented after the War, was far more generous than any of the downed Americans had promised but it surely made Ed and other downed Americans look pretty darned good!

Ed ran into both Polish and Russian prison camp escapees who were with the Italian Partisans. They were a big help to him since he spoke both Polish and Russian – vestiges of his ethnic heritage that now came in quite handy. He could, at least, speak and be understood. When he had healed for a few days, Ed began his journey south - back to the American troops.

Speaking Polish helped him immensely on his journey south. Hell, Ed even hitched a ride with a German convoy by claiming to be a Pole looking for work as a cook in the prison camps. Many Germans, it seemed, also spoke Polish and, of course, Ed played deaf if they tried to speak any English to him.

Basically, Ed walked south – the whole two hundred miles back to the Allied troops. It took him six weeks, but he did it. And he took off a lot of weight. He was two hundred and six pounds when we were shot down. He was a hundred and thirty-seven when he reached the Allied troops in early August.

While we tend to think of Americans as having done most of the fighting, there were a whole lot of other nations involved. Ed first hooked up with some Indians (from India, not American Indians), the Gurkas, who were fighting with the British and who were also moving up the Italian boot with the British and American front lines.

Ed hadn't changed his clothes from the time he left the Partisans until he reached the Allied troops. He just never felt safe enough to take them off even to bathe. It's amazing how vulnerable one feels with one's pants down or off. I can't say that I changed mine either. What you do enjoy when you're like that is finding a stream that is deep enough to wade in. You don't take anything off, not even your shoes; you just walk in, completely saturate yourself with water, and walk out. And you do feel a whole lot cleaner afterward.

Those clothes didn't fit him very well at the end with all the weight he had lost and after six weeks of walking, hiding, and sleeping in them. The Gurkas outfitted him with some British combat issue – most notably khaki Bermuda shorts – and shipped him back to Corsica. He got there on August 3rd, made out a report, visited with Holley and Semanak, and was shipped back to the U.S. a day later.

Chapter Nineteen
D-Day In Barberino di Mugello

September 9th was a day I had awaited for almost three months. I was awakened by the steady dripping of water on my leg from the rain overnight. A thin line of water slid down the underside of the stone lip of my cave and, when unable to hang on any longer, dropped down and splattered me. I lay there, listening, mentally surveying the start of another day. I had learned during these last three months to think first and then move cautiously.

The Americans entered the valley from the south. The Germans had cleared out the night before and there wasn't even any fire. I watched the Americans advance slowly -- being careful lest they be ambushed.

This might be the day and then again, it might not. There would be no large-scale fighting here, of that I was sure, but there could be any number of skirmishes. Slowly pulling aside the small limb, I saw that a thick dank fog had smothered the steep-sloped valley. That was good. No patrols would be moving until it lifted. I lay back, hardly bothering to move. I didn't think. I just lay there and listened; how long I did not know or care.

Gradually the sun burned the fog from the valley. Again I pulled back the limb and looked toward the other side. Men were gliding in and out of the heavy brush. It was a patrol, whose I did not know. Then I heard a mumbled curse. It sounded like, "For Christ's sake, Joe, shut up." I remained quiet. Where there was an American patrol there could be a German one as well, each stalking the other, shooting and then scampering away.

Suddenly the sharp staccato of German burp guns shattered the silence. Carbines quickly answered. Then all was still. An hour passed, then another. I pulled myself to my haunches. The valley would be clear of patrols by this time. It shouldn't have taken very long for both patrols to realize that this little, overgrown, valley was a potential death trap.

My white Italian sport shirt had been browned by the dirt of the hills. My gray wool pants were wet and rumpled and streaked with mud. I looked like a fugitive from Hell. Slowly, quietly, I moved down the mountain, not moving a leaf, not breaking a twig. Often I would stop and listen and listen and listen. Then I'd move on toward Beppe's small square Roman-type farm house that was down at the edge of the woods.

The dull heavy odors of the barnyard were matched by my month-old sweat. I squatted and watched. My Italian friends were drawn up into small groups and were speaking rapidly in quiet, subdued voices. Dina was sitting on the old gray stone wall, calm, serene and waiting. Beppe was standing near by. His brown-lined face was drawn tight with fear. Beppe was scared. There were still Germans around and with the Americans coming in, they could get caught in the crossfire. If trouble came Beppe could not be much help, but Beppe would not run.

I slid behind the old wall. No one had seen me except Dina. I motioned to her to be quiet. She got up and idly made her way around to me.

"Americani a qui," I whispered to her, "ma anche Teseschi." 'There are American patrols in the area, but also Germans.' Suddenly Renzo, the tall, gregarious blonde from Firenze saw me.

"Bon Giorno, Georgio! Bon Giorno!" he half-called and half-sang.

I hissed back: "Piano, Renzo! Piano!"

That broke the tension. It seems that the world was always saying "Piano, Renzo! Piano!" At once they were all around me. Some laughing, some crying, some pleading, but all talking as fast as they could.

Suddenly Dina shouted, "Piano." Just as with Beppe, when Dina spoke, everyone listened. The valley was instantly quiet again. Softly she told them that there were Americans near, but also Tedeschi.

Unexpectedly, there was a rustle of leaves. We all turned to see a thin line of brown clad soldiers glide from the midst of the trees. They were American G.I.'s.

I stepped from the group and slowly walked toward the soldiers.

"It's all right," I said, "I'm an American."

The carbine snapped to the Sergeant's shoulder. His finger tightened on the trigger. It was pointed at my head. The three months behind the lines had taught me well. There was no panic. I looked at the Sergeant and quietly said, "If you shoot, you better make sure you get me, because if you don't, I'll break your damn neck."

Never moving the gun the Sergeant barked. "Don't move, just stand there, I'll call the shots."

A Corporal ran up to me and quickly frisked my entire body.

"It's OK, Sarge, he's not armed."

"Who are you and what in the hell are you doing here?"

"I'm Lieutenant Harry D. George, 487th Bomb Squadron, 340th Bomb Group, 12th Air Force. I was shot down here three months ago during a raid on Gricigliano."

I was just getting ready to recite my serial number when the Sergeant asked to see my dog tags.

"I don't have them anymore. They were lost when I jumped." That wasn't true, but it made no difference to him.

"OK then. Where are you from?"

"Philadelphia."

"I'm from Philadelphia too. What part of the city?"

"Well, Sergeant, I'm not from the city of Philadelphia. I'm from a small town about 40 miles west, Coatesville, PA."

There was a deathly silence.

"My cousins live in Coatesville," the Sergeant continued, "and I spent some time there as a kid. They own the Coca-Cola bottling plant there. Do you know their name?"

"The Filoromos."

"They got any kids?"

"Three boys, Sam, Jim, and Joe."

"Well I'll be damned! Glad to meet you, Lieutenant. I'm Tony Scalio, Sir," and with that he lowered his rifle and came over and shook my hand. The other members of the patrol lowered theirs as well and the merriment began.

The mission had been accomplished! I had survived and would soon be back with my unit -- and maybe even bombing some more Germans.

My Italian friends had kept me from the 'Tedeschi' and that victory seemed as big as that of the Allies who were in the process of running them out of Italy. But my Italian friends were also sad. We had become very close and they would miss me very much. And I them.

There was no time for a bath, but there were clean clothes for me from Renzo -- a fresh shirt, new pants, and new two-toned shoes. I was soon a very stylish 'Georgio Italiano'! And a splash or two of Renzo's cologne helped my smell more than a little bit.

Once I was changed, there were hugs and kisses from everyone -- from Beppe, from Dina, from Nello and his Dina, from Renzo and Fernanda, from Lindo and Julia, from the children -- Graziella, Lina, and Bruna, even from young Gino who had been so tentative at first, but who was now my bosom buddy, from Mario, Nello's son, from Franca and Piero, Renzo and Fernanda's children, and from Bruna, Beppe's sister.

And on September 9th, there were pictures. The photos were taken openly now -- me with all the men, with all the women, with Beppe, with Nello and with Renzo. It was truly a glorious day! My day – *Georgio's Liberation Day*!

While we were taking the pictures, Dina and the wives brought out some food and wine for their liberators.

You know, I had some close calls in those three months behind the lines, but the only time I literally had a gun cocked and aimed at my head was at the hands of an American! I guess that Sergeant was just doing his job, but having an American point a gun a me really pissed me off! What if he hadn't had relatives in Coatesville? Would he have killed me?

Anyway, once the pictures were taken and the food consumed, the Sergeant and I talked a bit. There was so much to tell. The Sergeant couldn't believe that I had actually been there and survived without being captured for three months.

"It was all due to these courageous people," I told him. "They risked their lives for me -- quite literally every day since June 22nd. Every day!"

The Sergeant was impressed, but he had to move on. They had to scout the countryside for any remaining Germans. He told me that he would send someone for me shortly so that I could be returned to my unit.

Beppe pulled me aside and whispered something to me.

"Sergeant, before you go, I would suggest that we both go and pay a visit to the local Padrone. He OK'd what these people did and that should be acknowledged. It may help these people and I would really appreciate it if you would come with us to the Padrone's."

"Certainly, Lieutenant. Visiting him may help us as well."

It was time for good-byes to the families. The good-byes were hard and wonderful. There were no words for my feelings -- what could you say that could possibly show the love and admiration I felt for these people, these dear and very courageous people? Everyone cried. Everyone hugged. I kissed each of the women on the cheek and each of the children on the forehead. The tears were flowing everywhere. But it was time to leave.

The Sergeant called for two Jeeps and before long, they arrived. Beppe, Nello, Renzo and I crowded into one Jeep. The Sergeant and his patrol crowded into the other. We set out for the Padrone's.

The Padrone, Alphonso Manelli, greeted all of us at the door. Beppe introduced me and then the Sergeant to the Padrone. The Padrone greeted us both with a firm but reserved hug. The Padrone was a very dignified man probably in his 40's. He invited us all in and offered us some wine. No, Grappa would be better! So Grappa it was. It was a time for celebration. Everyone toasted me, then the Padrone. We toasted Beppe and Nello and Renzo. And we toasted the Sergeant and his troops.

The Padrone wanted the Sergeant to understand that Beppe and Nello and Renzo had helped me with his approval. He hoped that the Americans would remember this. Sergeant Scalio spoke fluent Italian so no interpreter was needed. The Sergeant told the Padrone that the American military appreciated all of their efforts and that he would make that part of his report to his commander. That pleased the Padrone and another round of Grappa was offered to all.

Quite frankly, I had several 'extra' rounds of Grappa. I was finally safe and celebrating with my friends and, perhaps, got just a bit carried away with the Grappa. It was *Georgio's Liberation Day* in Barberino di Mugello! And I was *Georgio*!

Then the Sergeant and his troops had to leave -- they did have to search the area for Germans. It felt good to have someone hunting for Germans instead of them hunting for me! The Sergeant told me that he would radio his commander and have me picked up. He said his good-byes and went outside and had his radio man call the Captain at their Headquarters which had been set up at the southern end of the valley.

"Captain, I've got an American pilot here who needs to be picked up and returned to his unit. He's been here since being shot down on June 22nd. We're at the big house along the main road through the valley -- at the Padrone's."

"Right, Sarge. I'll send a Jeep right over to pick him up."

"Ummm, Captain, I don't think he's in any shape to ride in a Jeep right now."

"'Roger. I can understand that after three months behind the lines. I'll send an ambulance. Over and out."

"Boy, the Captain's going to be surprised when this guy gets back half-looped instead of half-starved to death," the Sergeant muttered to himself. "Oh, what the hell, we haven't had any casualties all day and he's entitled." He climbed into the Jeep and sped off.

When the ambulance pulled up in front of the Padrone's, it was none too soon. I was drunk and completely overwhelmed with emotion. It was time for good-byes again, this time to Nello, Renzo and Beppe. Such intense emotion is not easy to handle. I did not know how to handle it -- and the Grappa wasn't helping. There were hugs -- each long, strong, and heartfelt. And tears. And many "mille grazie's." I wanted to go home, but I didn't want to or know how to say good-bye to these men either. But it was time.

As I got into the ambulance, Beppe came over, hugged me one last time and gave me his wallet. It was a beautiful, carved leather wallet and one I had seen and admired on several occasions. I'd never understood how wonderful Florentine leather work was until I had seen that wallet. But I also understood that it wasn't just a memento. I knew that Beppe's heart was in it. And it would go with me. And part of mine would always stay with him.

I regretted that I had nothing to give in return, but then, I had had nothing to give any of them from the day I arrived. I had learned to accept what was given and just be grateful for it. Our tear-filled eyes met one last time and I crawled into the ambulance.

"Ciao, Beppe."

"Ciao, Georgio."

The ambulance sped down the lane and took me back to the Americans.

Chapter Twenty
Anniversary Reunion

I was extremely lucky to get back – the American advance stalled about five miles north of Barberino di Mugello at the Futa Pass and then moved about another twenty miles north to where the German line of defense, the Gothic Line, remained for the entire winter of '44-'45. I doubt that I could have survived in those mountains through the winter.

My mother continued the story:

"After I received the MIA telegram, I found every day difficult. It was agonizing -- not knowing. I wrote to the Squadron and to Ferrell Holley, the pilot on Harry's original crew, on July 6th, the very day I received the MIA telegram. I heard nothing further until early August.

"The Army finally responded to my letters on August 5th. They sent me a letter stating that one chute had been seen to leave the plane – that was the first fact on which I could realistically base some hope.

"After I received the Army's letter, I called Betty Semenak. She had just heard from Joe.

"I had talked to Betty on the 6th of July when I received the first telegram. Betty had already received a letter and a cablegram from Joe. He told her to remember the date of June 22nd and not to worry about him – he was all right. He was worried that I would be notified by the War Department of Harry's being shot down and would then call Betty (which I did) before she knew that he was all right. He didn't want Betty to think that he had been shot down too.

"When I talked to Betty on August 9th, she read me the letter she had just received from Joe. It was dated July, 25th. He said that he had been on the same mission and that he had every reason to believe that Harry would come back OK. I think it was just a feeling, something on faith, but it was very good to hear. Someone who was there had reason to hope. That was important to me.

"Both Ferrell Holley and Joe Semenak wrote letters to me on August 22nd. They had just received my letter of July 6th! Ferrell said that he and Joe had wanted to write to me sooner, but that the Army was pretty strict about notification - the War Department had to be the first to notify family members. At that point, they knew that Ed had gotten back."

From Ferrel Holley:

>Dear Peg,
>
>... It was an afternoon mission and he got three of your letters just before take off. He was to fly with another of our friends that day that we had been with at Columbia. I was flying the ship not ten feet below him and right on his tail. There was flak, Peg; lots of it! But we were doing OK until a lucky hit found his ship – couldn't have been bad cause the ship went down for a few minutes under very good control. Several men left the ship; one whose chute didn't open, they think???
>
>No one was sure what went on until one of that crew made his way thru the lines and got back to the squadron after six weeks. I talked with him and he could only tell me what some Italians had told him. You see, he (the Boy who is back) was the first to leave the ship. The <u>odds</u> <u>sound</u> <u>very</u> <u>good</u> <u>to</u> <u>me</u>, Peg. And I only hope and pray they are right. Now we can only wait.
>
>As for the rest of us, we still don't like it, but we get along. Maybe we will all be back together before too long...
>
>Yours truly,
>
>Ferrell
>
>*The friend from Columbia and the "Boy who is back" was Ed Dombrowski.*

My mother continued:

"That letter was accompanied by a similarly eloquent letter from Joe Semenak.

"After those letters, I had even more hope. I knew what I felt on June 22nd on the hospital stairs – something bad had happened to Harry, but that he was not killed. That was very real. Now I had some concrete facts to support that feeling – some real basis for hope. But I was still afraid to hope too much.

"I immersed myself in my work at the hospital. That got me through the days and many of the nights. I worked as much as I physically could. Both Harry's family and mine rallied around me. I received letters from friends and relatives, near and far. All had the same problem – what can you say except not to give up hope?

"The most poignant letters were from Harry's maiden Aunt, Mary George. She was insistent that I not give up hope. I knew that she had been through the same thing in World War I. Her hopes had ultimately been dashed, but she knew what had to be done and that hope was the only thing to hang onto – until the situation was definitively resolved one way or the other.

"I hoped and I worked. And I accepted all of the good wishes and thoughts from friends and family. That's how I got through it.

"I received the telegram that he was all right on September 21$^{st.}$ I ran around the hospital telling everyone. I was deliriously happy. I went to Lancaster that evening to visit my family. We went to see 'Arsenic and Old Lace' at a local theater.

"Then I received three letters from him. I knew he would be coming home, I just didn't know when."

Tuesday, September 12, 1944

My Darling Margie,

At long last, dearest, I am once again able to write you. The Americans got here two days ago and I came down out of the mountains and believe me, I sure was glad to see them. I was behind the German lines for seventy-eight days and have had myself quite a time. For the present, I won't bother going into any details about my recent experience except that I am in good health and good shape. I am writing this in a house that is occupied by American soldiers and it sure is good to talk English again. My Italian vocabulary isn't half bad now and I can make my self understood and usually know what the Italians are talking about.

I want to tell you now, dearest, I owe my life to these Italian farmers. They have been wonderful to me. I intended to write yesterday, but I ran into a couple of fellows from Philadelphia and I guess I drank a little too much vino because at four o'clock in the afternoon, I went to bed and awoke this morning.

I imagine, dearest, that you have been terribly worried and that worried me, but now everything is all right again. Try and realize, dearest, that although the going may be rough sometimes, I'll get through and come back to you.

I was not flying with Holley and Semanak the day we were shot down, so I guess they are still O.K.

Here I am back again and now well behind the American lines and expect to be back to my base sometime tomorrow. What they will do with me then, I don't know, but it'll be swell just to be back again.

I had my first shower today and at the present feel like a new man. Honey, you can't realize how good it feels to be free again. I'm half afraid it's all a dream and I'll wake up and find myself back in the mountains.

Well, darling, I am going to get around to closing now and I'll write again tomorrow. Take care of yourself, honey and remember I love you more than life itself.

Your Loving Husband,

Harry

V-Mail
1st Lt. Harry D. George
487th Bomb Squadron, 340th Bomb Group

Italy, Sept. 15, 1944

My Dearest Margie,

Well, honey, here I am back again and let me say once more it sure is swell to be able to write you again. By the time you receive this, I imagine the War Dept. will have already notified you of my safe arrival back to the American lines. I wrote you a few days ago but as I was still at the front lines, it may take a little while for the letter to go through.

Yesterday, my darling, was quite a big day in your husband's little life. First, if you will scan the return address on this letter closely, you will note that it is now 1st Lt. instead of Second (getting up the world). Second, (I don't know whether you have been notified of this or not) I was awarded the Distinguished Flying Cross and the Air Medal. I darn near popped over when they told me that. Now for the third event, I shall print so that it will be perfectly clear: I am coming <u>HOME!</u> I pick up my orders this afternoon, go back to Corsica tomorrow, spend three days there and from then it is just a matter of waiting until they have space on a plane or a boat. Then a nice big thirty (30) day leave. Oh, honey, just think a whole month together.

I was back to Corsica for a few hours a couple of days ago and both Joe and Holley are fine. You should have seen the gang when they saw me. Darn near went wild.

In case you can hardly believe that this isn't all a dream, you may take time out and have someone pinch you. Well, honey, I think I'll close now as I want to get a few lines off to Beck. Do not write me as I expect to be on my way home before your mail would catch up with me. Also, arrange for a thirty day leave from the hospital for whenever I get there. In case you don't receive my other letter, I was never captured by the Germans but spent two and a half months behind the lines.

Your Loving Husband,

Harry

Wednesday, Sept. 27, 1944

Dearest Margie,

Well, honey, here's your husband back again. I am at a port of embarkation and just waiting around. I would sure like to beat this letter home, but don't have any idea whether I will or not. I was a little under the weather yesterday, had been eating too much candy, etc., so I just laid around and this morning I am back to normal and am feeling fine.

There really isn't anything new to write about dear, but just the realization that I will soon be back with you makes everything swell. I could start now and tell you how much I love you and am looking forward to being back with you and be able to love you again, but, honey, I'll be there in person before too long so will save it until I get there.

I believe I told you I would get 30 days leave. Well, I was wrong. It is a 21 day leave, but that is still good.

Well, dearest, I will close now. Take care of your lovely self and remember I'll soon be home.

Your Loving Husband,

Harry

My mother continued:

"I was talking to Laura George, my sister-in-law, when I knew definitely that Harry was coming home, and she very graciously said we were to stay at their place. (I had been living at the hospital and had no room suitable to the two of us.) French and Laura had a room all ready for us.

"On Friday, Oct. 13, 1944, I called Laura and she felt he would be home just any day and as they were going away for the weekend, she would leave the key to the house with Florence Wright across the street. And, although I was hoping, I just could not believe he would get home in time for our Fifth Anniversary – October 14th, 1944.

"On Sat., Oct., 14, 1944, at about 9:30 a.m., a call came for me "collect" from Cleveland, Ohio from your father. He had actually reached the States on our Fifth Wedding Anniversary! We talked and I pleaded to be allowed to meet him in Washington, his next stop. But at last, I was consoled with the idea that he would be home in 2 or 3 days. I was just too happy to work, but I went through the motions anyway and went off duty at 3 p.m. I went to town to get a ring for Harry's anniversary gift, and decided to buy another new dress.

"Then I went back to the hospital for supper and had just returned to the Nurses' Home when the phone rang. It was Western Union for me telling me to meet the 9:30 p.m. train (and it wasn't "collect" either) as it was possible for him to get home on our Anniversary. Needless to say, I was the happiest, most excited girl in the world.

"Although I tried to waste time, I was dressed in my newest finery long before train time. I then went down town to Wright's to get the door key and I sat there and talked for about a half-hour. When I got to the station, it was only 9:00 p.m. I had waited only a few minutes when Denny Slaymaker and Pauline Stauffer came to help me wait.

"The St. Louisan passed through Coatesville in two parts. One part stopped. The other didn't. They were made into one train in Harrisburg. The first part of the train flew by at about 100 miles an hour and I thought I saw Harry on it. I nearly had heart failure. It would just be like him to get on the wrong part.

"Then, shortly thereafter, the other part pulled in. As the train slowed, I looked in every window for him and couldn't see him. I was afraid that he had missed it entirely. Then the train finally stopped. There he was standing on the platform right in front of me.

"His first words were 'Hiya, Kid, Here I am.'"

"We couldn't move. We just stood there looking at each other...and looking....and looking and looking. People were going around him to the next stairway to get off. Finally, he started to step down."

My father interjected:

Yeah, and as soon as I was within reach, she started grabbing and feeling me from my ankles to...well, suffice it to say that I'm the only person who ever returned from war and got a complete physical *before* getting off the train!

And it was thorough!

I think she wanted to see what parts I had left and to make sure that they all worked!

"Harry!" Mom chided as she did on cue every time he told that story. "I wasn't just interested in THAT!"

"Not JUST that," was his reply, "but certainly IN that!"

Mom blushed, but there was nothing she could do. The story was true and she couldn't deny it.

"Your father insisted on driving the car home and he really was "off the beam," my mother added.

Yeah, I may have been 'off the beam' on the way home, but not once I got there! Some things you forget...and some things you don't!

My mother continued,

"When we got home, it was truly wonderful as we were alone and could celebrate our anniversary our own way. He brought me a lovely bracelet from Naples with three cameos on it. We looked at souvenirs and talked for ages. It certainly was grand to have him back."

Chapter Twenty-One
Sister Beck and Uncle Harold

The 21-day leave was grand and glorious! We had dinners out at the farm with Walt and Mary and the boys. We visited with just about anyone and everyone - family, friends, and many whom we didn't know, but who had read about my story in the paper. I was a local hero – one who had come back.

In November, I reported to the Southeast Training Command in Albany, Georgia to begin my time as an instructor. Then, in December, our euphoria ended when we received word that my sister, Beck, an Army nurse, had been killed in Africa on December 29th, 1944. She had served two tours of duty in Burma and India and was coming home on leave. She stopped in the Middle East for a few days and then caught a plane flying wounded soldiers back to the U.S. The plane she was in flew into a mountain in Africa in a dense fog. She was one of the few on that plane that they could even identify – and that was from her dental records.

Beck was eight years older than I and had been a wonderful sister. She had bought me my trombone with the first money she earned as a nurse. She always thought of others first. As high as I had been over surviving my ordeal and getting home, I was that low over Beck's death. But that's what war is - the random death of good people. There is no reason to it or why one survives and another doesn't. I had had fleeting thoughts of requesting a return to combat until Beck's death. That ended those thoughts for me. Our family had given enough.

But there were still some good times for us. After the leave, I was temporarily assigned to instructor's school at Brooks Field in San Antonio, Texas. I liked that town and your mother joined me there.

In July of 1945, I was assigned to the Air Transport Command (ATC) in Memphis to start ferrying planes to the Pacific Theater. I wasn't interested in flying planes any more. I would, of course, do it. I'd even go back into combat if necessary, but June 22nd had taken the luster away from flying airplanes for me. It wasn't the same and I wasn't the same.

We had a nice setup in Memphis which came about quite by accident. I was in the check-in line at Memphis along with a fellow pilot by the name of Edsel George. I had met Edsel during training and then we had run into him and his wife at a gas station on our drive from Albany, Georgia to Memphis. He had also just been transferred to the ATC.

The Major, who was checking us in, was quite obnoxious and filled up with his own importance. I never did like that type. The line was moving very slowly and I couldn't help but notice a huge portrait hanging on the wall of Lt. General Harold George, Commanding Officer of the Air Transport Command. I had never seen or heard of him.

I looked back at Edsel and said in a rather loud voice, "The next time I write Uncle Harold, I'm going to tell him what a screwed up mess his ATC really is."

Edsel immediately rose to the occasion. "Yeah," he said, "I half believed all the crap he used to feed us - but this is just as screwed up as the rest of the Army."

By this time, the officious Major was ready to check us in.

"You don't seem to like it here and yet you aren't even checked in, Lieutenant" he said as I stepped up to his desk.

"If you had listened to as much crap about how great the ATC was as I have from my Uncle, you'd probably feel the same way," I replied."

"And just who is your uncle, Lieutenant?"

"That's him," I replied, pointing to General George's portrait, "Uncle Harold, my namesake! And my cousin, Edsel George, another nephew, is here too!"

Well, the Major did an immediate about face. Never during my military life have I received such royal treatment as during my stay in Memphis! And did we play it to the hilt!

A table for four, for Edsel and me and our wives, was reserved for "The Georges" every night at the Officer's Club and the field personnel went all out to accommodate us at every turn. I never did have to ferry a plane anywhere. We were scheduled to begin ferrying planes to the Pacific shortly, but the dropping of the bombs on Hiroshima and Nagasaki made that unnecessary.

We were at the ATC in Memphis from July until the end of the war in August. Edsel and I were discharged two days later. Although I never met the General, I shall always be indebted to him. We had a great time in the ATC!

That's it. The end. The rest you know well.

The rest I do know well...and it follows.

Chapter Twenty-Two
Return To Italy

Through the years, my father and mother wrote to Beppe and Nello and Renzo and their families. Beppe and Renzo were both regular correspondents at first. My father tried to think of ways to repay his Italian friends in some way, but could never really come up with a good idea. They had talked about offering to bring little Gino to the U.S. to provide him with a good education, but that seemed like trying to steal Beppe's only son. And there would be no guarantee that they would be able to afford a college education for him. Then, in 1949, they had their own son, yours truly, and realized the importance of one's son to the family. The thoughts they had had of helping to educate Gino seemed very inappropriate.

Renzo and Fernanda had returned to Florence. She was a dress designer and they had established a factory to make her dresses. They re-opened their couturier shop in Florence and then opened ones in Rome and Paris. They wrote and tried to convince my parents to open ones for them in New York and Brazil. My father didn't want to be in the women's clothing business. He preferred the steel business and that was that.

Eventually, the frequency of the correspondence dwindled. My parents wrote to Beppe and Dina twice a year. The responses often took months because of the difficulty they had in getting them translated. And then my parents had to find people to translate Beppe and Dina's letters.

Their lives moved on. My father had gone back to work for the steel mill after the war and stayed there through 1960. He then changed jobs -- going with a slag processing firm in 1961. Then things started to change. The Company grew and he grew. He became Vice President of Operations. The company had operations in Pennsylvania, Ohio, New Jersey, California, and Mexico, Venezuela, and Brazil. He traveled frequently. Life was pretty darn good.

On July 31st 1968, the day before her 51st birthday, my mother had a heart attack. The initial prognosis was not good -- she would not likely live and if she did, she would likely only be a vegetable. She was comatose through the night, but the next morning, she started to speak. That was a good sign. She recovered fully.

That caused some re-thinking of their priorities. As soon as she was cleared by her doctors to travel, they were going to Italy. They could afford it and it was time. They would take me and my fiancee with them as well.

We flew to Rome and spent a few days sightseeing. While the sights were grand enough, my father was clearly anxious to get back to Barberino di Mugello. We took the train to Florence and spent several more anxious days there. Those were good days – again the sights were spectacular -- and gave my parents time to find an interpreter. We would need one in the country. My father remembered little or no Italian -- and, hopefully, 'scapare,' the one word which was indelibly etched into his brain, would not be needed this time.

Then the day came, the day when he would be reunited with his friends in Italy. The interpreter arrived with a Fiat limousine and we left downtown Florence for Galliano di Mugello, the town where Beppe and Dina lived in 1969. Galliano is about five miles east of Barberino.

In half an hour, we pulled into the town. When the interpreter stopped in the town square to get directions to Beppe's, it seemed that every window and doorway filled with friendly faces. Everyone knew we were coming! We were close and had only to drive back to the edge of town.

As we pulled up to the farmhouse, Beppe and Dina's family all greeted us -- and then there was Dina. A brief cry of 'Georgio' and several tear-filled hugs later, 'Georgio' asked Dina where Beppe was. He was down in one of the farm buildings. We all started to walk in that direction.

Beppe had heard the commotion and had started up toward the house. As the two neared each other, the rest of us dropped back. The two slender men, each with angular features and deliberate walks, got closer. They seemed very much alike, these two -- purposeful and dignified -- very much like brothers. At twenty feet there were smiles, big smiles. At ten feet, there were tears of joy, streams of them. Their arms opened and there was a hug, a hug that only two comrades and heroes who admired each other with every ounce of their beings could know but which enveloped all who there. My father may have been very disciplined and emotionally controlled at home, but in Italy, he was 'Georgio' - very emotional and *very* Italian. He was *Georgio Italiano*.

Similar reunions followed with Nello and Renzo and their families.

Beppe came with us to Barberino di Mugello to see Nello. There was no answer at the door to his apartment so we went to his son's barber shop, a short distance down street in the same block. Mario, Nello's son, was thrilled and called his father. Nello came home in less than five minutes and his wife, Dina, shortly thereafter. There were, of course, warm hugs and then Nello started talking.

As was to be the case often over the next five days, the interpreter, Vittorio Sulli, became so engrossed in listening to the stories that he forgot to translate for us. But a gentle prod always brought him back. We sat around Nello's dining room table for several hours talking and toasting. The same ease that my father had with Beppe was clearly also there with Nello.

The visit with Renzo was shorter. Beppe took us to the newspaper store Renzo owned at the North Florence stop on the Autostrada. Fernanda ran the dress design and manufacturing business while Renzo helped with that business and ran the shop. Renzo was the most changed of the four. He had put on a lot of weight. But he recognized my father instantly, cried, and gave him a big hug.

Roughly translated, Renzo explained his size this way. "My family -- they tell me, 'Renzo, you eat too much. Renzo, you drink too much. And Renzo, you smoke too much.' But I tell them this...you can't live too much and I know how to live!"

He called Fernanda and she came out from Florence to join the reunion. We adjourned to a local restaurant for a few drinks and some more stories.

The remaining days at Beppe's were filled with parties from early morning until late at night. Visitors from both Barberino and Galliano streamed into and out of Beppe and Dina's house for the entire length of our stay – hundreds of them! The local Chief of Police stopped by and offered us the use of his police car for the duration of our visit. The interpreter, Vittorio Sulli, continued to get lost in the stories. One of us would then nudge him and he would then try to digest everything that had been said in the previous fifteen minutes. Vittorio was having a high old time as well.

Beppe's brother, Lindo, and sister-in-law, Julia, were there with their two sons, Mauro and Juliano and teenage daughter, Patrizia. Both families, Beppe's and Lindo's, lived in the same huge farmhouse. Mealtime was very Italian - fourteen people gathered around the huge table. It was a different culture, but a very good and sociable one.

Lindo's son, Mauro, was in the Italian Air Force at the time. Mauro came home for our visit. He and Georgio talked Air Force when they could, but there was little time with all the visitors. Doriana, Lindo and Julia's baby who was born during the war, came home to visit with her husband, Renato, and their son, Fabrizio. Lindo's son, Juliano, was my age. We became friends and traveled in his car wherever the caravan went. I quickly came to understand how difficult it was to communicate in a language other than your own. But, as my father and Beppe had done years before, we did learn to communicate...and reasonably well.

Gino, Beppe's son, was now a grown man with a wife and three children of his own. Gino was a young, pleasant, and robust man with an ease about him very similar to Beppe's. His wife, Elena, was charming and Dina's aide-de-camp in the kitchen. The children, Sauro, looked like a little Gino, and Cinzia and Antonella, were cute and charming little girls.

Beppe's daughters, Lina and Graziella, had married and moved away. We visited both. The third daughter, Bruna, was still at home. And there was Beppe's Aunt, Rosa, aging and bent, and perennially parked on a chair in the kitchen – but not quiet. Zia Rosa always had comments on everything – especially on preparation of the meals. It was a large and bustling household! An obviously, a very happy one.

We toured the farm where the Ferri families all lived and worked. It was miraculous! They raised chickens (for eggs) and pigs. I forget the numbers, but there were something on the order of 40,000 chickens and 5000 pigs. The entire operation was automated - a technological marvel of the first order. Things had changed radically in Italy in the twenty-five years since the war. While America was forging ahead with the space program and would soon land a man on the moon, I felt a little backward – we didn't have farms like this back home in 1969, at least not that I had ever seen.

And there was Beppe's garden adjacent to the house. We would call it a field, but there, it was just a garden – where the produce for the family was grown.

With all the visitors came the pictures -- all the wartime pictures! Every man in Barberino di Mugello it seemed carried a picture of himself and 'Georgio' in his wallet – even twenty-five years after the War. It was gratifying to be adopted and loved by a whole town that just wanted to help an American. And each of those men, of course, expected Georgio to have a drink with them – which he did, but only wine this time, not Grappa, which he left for those who could handle it.

When Nello came over to Beppe's, we all made a trip back to the first cave. It was time for another picture of the three of them - twenty-five years later!

We made a visit to the Padrone's. Sergeant Scalio had been good to his word and reported to the American C/O that the Padrone and those who worked for him had assisted a downed American pilot. There was a certificate of appreciation from the U.S. Government hanging on the Padrone's wall to prove it.

On Sunday, Nello and his family hosted a grand dinner for us in a restaurant in Barberino di Mugello. Vittorio, the interpreter, worked overtime on that one.

When the time came to depart for what proved to be his final time, 'Georgio' and Beppe and Dina parted as they had been reunited -- amid hugs and tears, but also amid cheers, and countless 'Ciaos' and 'Arrivedercis' and more hugs -- and thankful that fate had, in a strange and difficult, but beautiful way, brought them together – once in war and now in peace.

Chapter Twenty-Three
The Measure Of A Woman

The social focal point of the town where we lived when I was young was the American Legion. Saturday nights were spent there - at least until the mid-1950's. They had a band or combo that played all kinds of music -- from standard 40's and 50's fare to polkas. That's where we went, not every Saturday night, but most of them. That's what families did back then.

I played pinball and occasionally watched my parents dance. I was always amazed at how graceful my somewhat gawky, six-foot-one father and my diminutive, five-foot-two mother were on the dance floor. Fred Astair and Ginger Rogers? Not quite, but not that far off either. I'm even told that I danced with all the little girls - mostly polkas - because anyone can hop around rhythmically and look like they're dancing the polka. But that's where we went on Saturday nights. To the American Legion.

That meant that my father had to belong to the Legion. And that meant we got *American Legion* magazine. I liked the comics. They were clean and funny. I didn't understand clean or its opposite at that age, but I understood funny and that they were. My father read the articles. I read the comics.

My father maintained his membership in the Parkesburg, Pa. American Legion long after the times changed and we moved away. He sent them a check once a year and they sent him magazines. They did some good things for vets and his money would help. That was it. I don't think any of us ever set foot in another American Legion after the mid-fifties. Times changed.

My mother, however, became intrigued with the ads in the back of the magazine – the ones plugging reunions of service groups. She watched them for years and finally, sometime in the late 60's or early 70's, saw one for his unit, the 57th Bomb Wing. She suggested that they attend one. My father said no.

He had only been in combat for 30 days. He barely knew anyone in the Squadron. A reunion? With whom?

He and my mother had tried to find Ed Dombrowski after the War to say 'thanks' for getting the escape hatch open and saving his life, but none of their letters were answered or returned. There was no point to going to any reunion. And that was that.

In 1973, however, things changed. My mother won the argument. (We called them 'debates' in our house, but arguments is what they were.) The reunion of the 57th Bomb Wing was being held in San Antonio. They had both liked the town when they were stationed there in 1945. Even if the reunion were a complete bust, and my father knew it would be, they could enjoy the town. He always liked the Alamo, anyway. So that year, they went.

The Reunion was nice enough. There were some great people - other B-25 pilots and ground crews. People who knew. People who understood what the war was. But there was no one there from his Squadron, the 487th. No one. Reunion? As he had told my mother, with whom? You can't have a reunion of one. So they enjoyed San Antone and that was that.

Well, that wasn't that. Not for my mother. She made a few calls and got a list of men who had served in the 487th through mid-1944 - about 400 men. The list had their 1944 addresses. She was off and running.

The measure of a woman?

She wrote. She phoned. And one by one she started tracking them down. Within a year, she had located 60 or so and strong-armed 30 or 40 of them into coming to the 1974 57th Bomb Wing Reunion in Williamsburg, Va. So, guess what? She and my father went to that one as well. As did I.

My parents got to know the 30 or 40 men and their wives from the 487th that Mom had contacted. I say 'Mom contacted' because, basically, she did all the talking. My father was always on the phone too, but he was just on the phone because he had been there - in the 487th on Corsica. All he ever said was that he was there for thirty days and didn't know anyone, but that

Mom was trying to reunite the Squadron. She had made it her mission in life and they should listen. She had a lot to say.

I tagged along for some of those meetings with 487th guys. They were fun. I heard more funny war stories over those four days than I had ever heard in my life - before or since. They didn't talk about combat at all. There was little point. They talked about the anomalies – and those were many.

Life in the 340th on Corsica wasn't all blood and guts. There were, indeed, fun times. The extra time, the time when they were not flying missions, had to be filled somehow. While they were men when they crawled into airplanes and bombed the Germans, they were boys a lot of the time too. They played, perhaps not a lot, but enough to relieve the stress that shooting and being shot at and seeing your buddies die or go down created. There were some darn funny tales!

I couldn't help but notice that there was an ease among these men, and with my father, that I had never seen before. It was like they were family, but closer. Easier. Even if they didn't know each other personally during the war, they understood each other perfectly and each admired and respected all of the others – regardless of rank, regardless of duty. That I found to be remarkable – as I had always imagined it was and should be, but actually, it was far better in the reality than it had ever been in my imagination.

One late afternoon, I walked into the ballroom where they all seemed to congregate when there were no scheduled activities. I noticed a tall man sitting at a table all alone. He had long black hair which hung halfway down his back. This was a crew-cut crowd and he stood out. And he was alone. With my beard and longish hair, I thought that perhaps I could put him at ease. I went over and introduced myself and sat down.

For the life of me, I can't remember his name, but what I do remember is that he was a Native American, 'The Chief' my father had mentioned. I think he was a real Chief by then or in line to become one in the tribal hierarchy. Regardless, we talked. He didn't feel he belonged there. He wasn't a pilot, wasn't a bombardier. He was just a guy who went over there and did his job and came home. The reunions, he thought, were for the pilots and flight crews. Not him.

I knew better. I had heard my mother talk to other members of the ground crews on the phone. These reunions were for everyone - regardless of rank or duty. I told him that and took him to meet my parents. And they took him to meet some other men from his Squadron. And it worked. The last I saw him, he was sitting at a full table, smiling and laughing, and having a high old time. I was now alone at the table, but that was fine. I'd leech on somewhere and do some more listening when the spirit moved me.

That Reunion in 1974 was a success for my mother and like most successes in life, one begets another. It whetted her whistle to find more men of the 487th. When they returned home after the reunion, she went right back at it and by 1976, she had located several hundred.

As the list grew, there was a need for the men to have some way to get in touch with each other. The Wing put out a newsletter which listed new members' addresses, but many of the men she found weren't interested in the Wing. It was too big, too far beyond their experience. They were part of the 487th and that's where their identity stopped. So she started publishing a quarterly newsletter for them, *The Men Of The 487th*.

The Squadron newsletter was not all that different from the Christmas letters many people now send - what's up with so-and-so, this person has moved and here's the new address and phone number, but it occasionally would contain a story or tidbit about the unit's combat service. The men loved the newsletter...and her for it. It was theirs.

My parents funded it out of their pocket and, on a retirement income, that was not always easy. My father would never have asked anyone for assistance and would have gone to his grave by his own hand before asking anyone for a nickel, but my mother had no qualms about it. Some help was needed and that was that.

At the next reunion, she put out a kitty bowl in their hospitality suite for the Squadron to help support the newsletter. She seeded the bowl with a couple of ones. She got 50's and 100's and checks. The newsletter never cost them much after that. Someone would always ask how the expenses were going and she'd either tell them that things were covered for now or they were tight. When they were tight, someone always gave them a hit - sometimes a big hit. The biggest hitter, and a silent an anonymous one, was my father's original bombardier, Joe Semenak. He'd hit Ascension Island dead on and been quite OK with Pop ever since...and then even more so.

And the men started sending her things: mission photos, copies of orders and personnel rosters, copies of their stories, pictures (I still have bags full of pictures), personal logs and journals. To many of them, she was the focal point of the Squadron. Her phone never stopped ringing. There were new leads phoned in and phone calls just to catch up. And there were letters. Lots of letters. All with tidbits about the War and the authors' service...or their gout. Personal stuff. To her!

So she kept going on tracking men down and publishing the newsletter. By the time she died in 1997, she had tracked down about 600 of the 900 who had served in the 487th during the War and published the newsletter for eighteen years. Not bad. Not bad at all.

As Paul Tibbets, pilot of the *Enola Gay* pointed out so eloquently in Bob Greene's book, *Duty*, the War was a special time for all who served. It wasn't that the War was great or the best of times. In many ways it was the antithesis of those. It was, however, the one time in each man's life where he stood as a man among men. That doesn't happen on football fields, or basketball courts, or in academia, or in business. It happens in war. For that reason, that time in the service, the time at war, was special to those who had been there. My mother's efforts to reunite the men of the 487th and to encourage them to continue to interact with the men with whom they stood as a man among men was greatly appreciated by all of them. She understood it and they knew that she did.

The measure of a woman?

Her efforts in reuniting the men of the 487th were so appreciated by them that when they donated the Squadron's Monument to the Air Force Museum at Wright-Patterson Air Force Base in Dayton, Ohio in 1987, they asked her to make the presentation for them. Now that's an honor! That's appreciation! And she did. My short, little, aging mother who had never flown in a B-25, never gone into combat, and never enlisted in the service presented the 487th Bomb Squadron's Monument to the Air Force Museum. She was the first woman to make such a presentation from a combat unit and the first non-military person to do so.

The measure of a woman?

As the men of the 487th and their wives started aging, long trips became difficult. So my mother instituted mini-regional reunions. They were nothing elaborate - just a hundred or so friends gathering at hotels which were within one day's driving distance. She started them in the east and before long, others were running similar affairs all across the country. They proved to be big hits as well.

My father always made the comment that when he married my mother, the Army lost a great general. He was being facetious, of course, but only about half. She could organize anything and after the War, she organized the 487th. Command structure be damned, she became their de-facto General (General Knapp, the real commander, a flier of note who had received his license from the Wright Brothers and who had been involved in choosing the crews for Doolittle's Raiders, notwithstanding). She was also their post-war Ernie Pyle. I guess my father had not been all that facetious after all. She didn't miss her calling, she just came to it later in life.

At their 50th Anniversary Party, my father highlighted her efforts with the 487th, "She's the one who reunited me with the men with whom, when the chips were down, you lived or died...and for that I honor her.. And the men of the 487th? Well, they think even more of her than I do! And that's a lot!"

The measure of a woman?

My mother, of course, returned to her first calling, nursing, when my father became ill. She did a great job at that too. That was hard. Her husband and the love of her life was dying. But she knew nursing. That's what she did and what she was.

She had become one at twenty and by twenty-seven, when my father was overseas, was running the nursing staff of the local hospital and training the student nurses. And then she taught home nursing to Homemakers, Inc., a hospice care service in Pennsylvania where she served on the Board of Directors for twenty years. She wrote their home care manual too – in her spare time. She knew nursing when it was more than just administering medications and looking at monitors. She knew bed pans, changing a bed with the patient in it, IV's, OR, and the delivery room, and so on. And more than anything, she knew how to give care. And all of that she gave to my father in his last months. He got the best of care – he got her.

When she ran out of gas at the end -- my father's last five days -- she knew to call for some hospice assistance and how to get out of the way. But for five long months, she did the hard tasks when it counted – all of them. She was there for him. And that made all the difference in the world.

After my father died, my mother came to live with me. That was hard, in part. An adjustment. But it had to be. And it was good. We became friends too. Good friends. Best of friends, actually. And she continued with the newsletter until her dying day, January 3, 1997.

She also continued to go to reunions during her time living with me. She found the travel part hard. She'd always opt out at the last minute and say she wasn't going to go. And I did what my father did when she got into one of her "I can't" modes - I kicked her you-know-what and made her go.

"I get disoriented," she'd say.

"So make all of your arrangements first. Make a list and follow it. You know how to do that. You taught me!"

So she went. She was getting old and infirm. But she went.

She made the arrangements for her flights, for the golf-cart rides to and from the gates, for someone to meet her and get her to the hotel. But she went. She made her lists and followed them.

She was needed at the reunions and she needed to go to them – to greet her boys, the Men Of The 487th. Sure there were tears when she'd meet one of Pop's closest buddies. But the tears passed. And she needed to do some crying anyway. Grieving for a husband of fifty years isn't over in a week or a month or a year. And she kept finding new Squadron members and had to meet them and their wives.

The measure of a woman? Not a bad yardstick, my mother, Margie. Or Dina. Or Beck.

Chapter Twenty-Four
Ed and I - One Last Time

In 1976, my mother was working the registration desk at the 57th Bomb Wing Reunion in Innisbrook, Florida. She wanted to work the registration desk to meet "her boys" when they came in.

A large well-dressed man came up to the desk and asked how one registered for the reunion. Margie handed him the registration card and told him that the fee was $50 – and that covered everything including the Saturday-night banquet. He took the card to an adjoining table and filled it out. He brought it back to her.

When she read the name, Edward P. Dombrowski, she shrieked and started to cry. They had been sending letters to Ed since 1945 with no response – and here he was standing right in front of her. Even though she had never met him, she ran around the table and gave him a big hug and kiss.

Ed had never received any of the letters. He was dumb-struck by my mother's reception. He hadn't expected anything like this and certainly not at the registration desk! He had eventually learned that it was Obravatz who had seen the Italian doctor and had come to conclude that my father was dead. There had never been any word about my father -- certainly none before Ed was shipped back to the States. All he knew was that he had seen my father's chute far below his. 'You mean he's been dead all these years and you're still carrying a torch and coming to reunions?' he asked Mom.

"No, Ed. Harry's alive! Very much alive! We've been searching for you for years!"

Tears filled Ed's eyes. He hadn't been sure whether this reunion thing was a good idea, but now it looked like it just might be. He had enjoyed Harry during the war even if they had only known each other for a brief time.

Then he started remembering that day -- June 22nd, 1944 when they were shot down over Italy. Those weren't pleasant memories. It was Ed's regular crew and they lost Casey, Ahlstrom and Kaplan -- good guys. Good friends.

My father was playing golf, but he would likely stop in the pro shop at the end of the first nine. Ed parked in the bar next to the pro shop and had a drink.

Ed sat there nervous as a kitten. And then he saw Harry enter the pro shop. He recognized Harry immediately. He called Harry's name and went to give him a hug. Harry didn't recognize him and stiff-armed him gently. Ed was disappointed that Harry didn't recognize him.

"Harry, it's me – Ed! Ed Dombrowski," Ed said.

That caught my father by complete surprise. He had long since given up on ever finding Ed. He looked -- it *was* Ed! He had been waiting for this moment for a long time. He looked at Ed again. Geez, it really was him!

The stiff arm went down and he hugged Ed hard. There were smiles and tears -- and more hugs. Hardly what one would expect from two middle-aged American men.

My father was thrilled to see Ed again and to actually say 'Thank you' – which he must have said several dozen times that afternoon. Ed was thrilled as well. And returned the 'Thank you.'

The two were inseparable for the duration of the reunion. They went everywhere -- sometimes with Ed's arm on my father's shoulder and sometimes with my father's arm on Ed's -- but always together.

The two became close friends that day and remained so thereafter – attending all subsequent Bomb Wing Reunions together with their wives and keeping in close touch in between.

In October of 1989, my father publicly thanked Ed for saving his life one more time. It was at my parents' 50th Anniversary Party.

After he and my mother were toasted, my father took the microphone. After a speech praising my mother and their fifty years of marriage, he introduced

Ed to his family and friends.

"Ed and I were in the 487th Squadron together in the War. In fact, after the War, I even wrote a story about that. And, as Ed so aptly puts it, I named the story after him, 'Ed and I,' but then wrote it entirely about myself."

"But," he continued in a more serious tone, "it was Ed who saved my life on June 22nd, 1944 and for that I owe him my life thereafter. I owe him a great thanks. He was a real hero that day. He went into the fire, suffered serious burns but got the hatch open so that we could escape. He's great and I love him."

"There aren't too many times when one is afforded the opportunity to express such thanks – or to do so publicly. I have been lucky enough to do so once when we were reunited in 1976 and I will do so again tonight. 'Thanks, Ed.' Stand up and take a bow. You earned it!"

Ed stood.

The applause, a standing ovation actually, from my parents and their family and friends was quite warm -- and quite befitting a very deserving war hero – even if he hadn't defeated Joe Louis in the second round.

Postscript

On Memorial Day, 1990, two other WW II vets, Frank Gaska and Kirk John, visited my father. They had known my father for most of their lives and knew his condition. Their visit was most appreciated. My father appreciated everything by then – every moment, every contact, every flower, every tree, and every sunrise. He especially appreciated a visit from two other vets on his last Memorial Day.

Not much was said. Not much had to be. They understood. So did he.

They talked a little about the war. They remembered that he had been shot down, but little beyond that. He answered a few of their questions about his service. Telling his story or any part of it was out of the question. Talking was getting increasingly difficult for him. So, for awhile, they just sat -- two vets honoring a third with a visit on his last Memorial Day.

Characteristically, as they rose to leave, my father reminded them to remember and honor his sister, Beck, as well. That was the point – to honor those who gave their lives in service to their country.

Frank and Kirk remembered Beck from their childhoods, but they had long since forgotten about her death in the war. They promised to continue to remember and honor her as well.

By the end of the first week of June, my mother was near exhaustion from the five-month ordeal. She needed some help. She called Homemaker's, the hospice service where she had served on the Board. They sent a nurse almost immediately.

The hospice nurse was of Italian descent. My mother mentioned my father's connection with Italy to her and she was quite intrigued. I was in the bedroom when the hospice nurse first came in. She asked him a few questions as she went about her work.

My father kept his responses to her questions very short. There was a gap between what he was able to convey and what she wanted to know. After the third or fourth question, I noticed his eyes looking to me for the response so I answered in his stead.

I started telling the story just as I had just heard it over the preceding four and half months – or at least the parts of if that were responsive to her question.

When I finished, I looked at him and asked him if I had gotten it right. A big smile and nod were his answers. "Very right," he whispered, "You have listened very well."

As his days played out, that routine with the hospice nurse was repeated any number of times, each with the same ending. Those smiles at the end of my tellings of parts of his story were some of the few smiles he smiled during his last days. I was pleased to have been the cause of them.

My father only made two final requests of me - to take care of my mother and to continue to tell his story. The first has been accomplished and, since you have gotten this far, now, so has the second.

My father refused the morphine that the doctor recommended for his last days. He wasn't going to go out with his mind fuzzy or without being in control. On the one hand, he was ready to go; on the other, he wanted to experience every second of life fully cognizant. He wanted every last second of it.

It was June 10th when the end seemed to be momentarily at hand. That was unfortunate because it was my daughter, Jen's, birthday. He had ceased talking by then, but did make eye contact and did respond to hand holding. He and I had a little meeting that morning. Alone.

I told him what the date and day were. I also told him that I didn't think he would want Jen's birthday forever clouded with his death. He closed and opened his eyes. He understood.

That evening, he slipped into a coma. His body steeled itself just as it had done when he determinedly wrestled 7C in his sleep years before, but he made it to the next morning - on auto-pilot.

On June 11, 1990, my fathers, Harry and 'Georgio' died.

The funeral services were neither special nor extraordinary. They were fitting and proper. My son, Harry, III, thirteen by then, proudly stood with me at the head of the casket at the viewing. He also joined me as one of the pall bearers. He would have it no other way. He too was his grandfather's grandson.

In 1995, I took my mother back to visit Beppe and Dina in Galliano. Mom was 78 and Beppe and Dina in their 90's. It was a wonderful visit even without 'Georgio.'

Beppe and Dina's grandson, Sauro (Gino's son), had married Pina Zito, a language teacher who is fluent in four languages, including English. While she couldn't be there all the time, she spent much of those five days interpreting for Mom, Beppe and Dina -- and for me in the evenings. All were in reasonably good health and just enjoyed being in each other's company. Unfortunately, Gino, my Italian couterpart, had been killed in an automobile accident several years before.

We spent the evenings gathered around the table with much of the family present. There were, of course, Beppe and Dina at opposite head ends of the table, Beppe's daughter, Bruna, my mother and I, Gino's widow, Elena, and her friend, Eduardo, and Elena's and Gino's children, Sauro with wife, Pina, Cinzia with her husband, Paolo Pieri, and Antonella with her husband, Claudio and their charming eight-year-old son, Lorenzo.

I spent my days exploring -- locating the key sites in my father's story: the house where Beppe had lived during the war, where the plane crashed (the Germans had salvaged it for the metal almost instantly), where the railroad bridge at Gricigliana was, and how everything fit together. We had done some of that in 1969 with my father, but I wanted to understand more, to have more details. So I explored during the daylight hours.

I also took part of one day and visited the American Military Cemetery just south of Florence, where my father's sister, my Aunt Beck, Lt. Rebecca L. George, is buried. For those who have never visited one of these sites -- and there are some 20 of them around the world -- they are absolutely beautiful and incredibly moving. (A list of them is enclosed.) They are immaculately maintained -- picture perfect for those friends and relatives who just might drop by. I strongly recommend making a half-day side trip to one of these cemeteries whenever one is overseas. There are more than 130,000 Americans buried in those 20 cemeteries and another 60,000 MIA who are memorialized there. Their sacrifices were no less than those whom we honor with ceremonies and parades at home. They should not be forgotten -- by any of us. A half-day side trip is little imposition and, in my opinion, will add quite a bit of perspective to any trip.

We had lost track of Nello and Renzo. Beppe had advised us upon our arrival that Nello and Nello's wife, Dina, were both deceased. He believed that Renzo and Fernanda were also deceased, but was not sure.

I thought that I remembered the location of Renzo's newspaper shop along the Autostrada where we had first visited Fernanda and him in 1969. I stopped there when returning from the cemetery on the off-chance the someone there might know something about him. His son, Piero, was behind the counter. Despite a complete lack of knowledge of each other's language, we had a delightful reunion as well as a few beers at a local bistro. Renzo and Fernanda were, in fact, deceased. I took Piero's address and gave him mine. We vowed to keep in touch.

On the '95 trip, Beppe offered to take me up on the mountain to the second cave. I didn't want to go (for health reasons), but figured that if a 92-year-old man who had saved my father's life wanted to take me up the mountain, I was obliged to follow.

Beppe, his grandson, Sauro, and grandson-in-law, Claudio, and I spent half a day climbing "Georgio's Mountain" ('Monte Georgio,' in Italian) in search of the second cave. At 92, Beppe led the way. The rest of us kept up as best we could. Beppe, I learned that day, was apparently part mountain goat -- even more agile on that mountain than he was at home -- and at 92 he was still an active bicycler and gardener. He climbed around that mountain like a 30-year old, or less. I had trouble at half his age.

It was then that I understood the paths made by the water runoff, the thickness of the brush, and the difficulty of finding anything or anyone on that mountain. Finally, tired and winded, I parked in a clearing about 80% of the way to the summit close to where Beppe remembered the second cave being. He and the others searched further. We never did find the cave (50 years can change a lot of things on a mountain), but quite frankly, as much as I would have loved to have visited it, I was quite content to sit there and take in the view of the valley -- the view my father had seen almost every day for three months 51 years earlier. It was spectacular! It felt like home.

After five days, the time came for us to take our leave. The partings were difficult, as they always were. In all likelihood, there would be no more visits or partings of principals -- only their offspring and their offsprings' offspring. But the partings were warm -- warm as only Italian partings with long histories can be.

My mother died in January of 1997. Beppe died the next year. Beppe's wife, Dina, wonderful and courageous Dina, is still alive as of this writing, as is Ed Dombrowski.

My father's Air Medal and The Distinguished Flying Cross that he earned on June 22, 1944 remain where they have always been -- in a safety deposit box at the bank. While the medals are important because of what they represent, what is more important is that his story and the stories of his heroes have not been and will not be forgotten.

Thank you for listening.

ISBN 1552125386